Arcadian Grace

Arcadian Grace

Stephen Falconer

RESOURCE *Publications* · Eugene, Oregon

ARCADIAN GRACE

Copyright © 2021 Stephen Falconer. All rights reserved. Except for brief quotations in critical publications or reviews, no part of this book may be reproduced in any manner without prior written permission from the publisher. Write: Permissions, Wipf and Stock Publishers, 199 W. 8th Ave., Suite 3, Eugene, OR 97401.

Resource Publications
An Imprint of Wipf and Stock Publishers
199 W. 8th Ave., Suite 3
Eugene, OR 97401

www.wipfandstock.com

PAPERBACK ISBN: 978-1-6667-3131-6
HARDCOVER ISBN: 978-1-6667-2368-7
EBOOK ISBN: 978-1-6667-2369-4

SEPTEMBER 13, 2021

The poems "Afterlife", "A New Dawn", and "To the Far Ends of the Earth" were previously printed in Camphill Correspondence, Chatham, New York

Contents

1 Where I Belong | 1
2 Poetic Faith | 2
3 The Outer Limit | 3
4 Mortal | 5
5 Hero | 7
6 All or Nothing | 8
7 At First Glance | 9
8 Earthbound | 10
9 Between the Earth and Cessation of Carnal Imagery | 11
10 Aflame | 14
11 Sun God | 16
12 Afterlife | 18
13 Over the Hill | 20
14 Fingertips Seeking the Star's Goodwill | 22
15 No Known End | 24
16 Arcadian Grace | 26
17 A Long Way Down | 27
18 Indivisible | 29
19 Centaur | 30
20 Fruit | 32
21 Mortification | 34
22 Awakening | 36
23 Heritage | 37
24 Revival | 38
25 Virtual Death | 40
26 Pieta | 42
27 A Personal Inclination | 44
28 Gnosis | 46
29 High Priestess | 48
30 At Home | 49
31 Guardian of Forgotten Kingdoms | 51
32 Goddess | 53
33 Enrichment | 54
34 Deliverance | 56
35 A Detached Point of View | 58
36 To the Far Ends of the Earth | 60
37 Mission | 62
38 The Great Architect | 64
39 Beneath the Cross | 66
40 Tranquility | 69
41 Art is its Own Reward | 71
42 Pilgrim | 73
43 Pillage | 75
44 Alms | 76
45 Grey Stone Winter | 78
46 A Glorious Enterprise | 79
47 Soon to Be Free | 81
48 A Lute Player's Homage | 84

| 49 | Betrothal | 85
| 50 | Release | 87
| 51 | From the Diary of Brother Simon | 88
| 52 | A Word for All | 91
| 53 | The Grass, the Trees, and Rivers | 92
| 54 | A New Order is Formed in the Temple | 93
| 55 | The Doge Recognizes a New Form of Entertainment | 95
| 56 | Masterpiece | 99
| 57 | Angel | 101
| 58 | Profundity | 103
| 59 | Work of Art | 105
| 60 | Now to Work | 107
| 61 | Luminous Night | 109
| 62 | Blessed Release | 110
| 63 | Heliocentric | 112
| 64 | A Humanist's Aspiration | 114
| 65 | An Artist's Tool | 115
| 66 | Fruits of the Spirit | 116
| 67 | Out of Reach | 118
| 68 | The Mirror Held Up to Sanity | 119
| 69 | Self-Perpetuation | 121
| 70 | Heretical | 123
| 71 | Immanence | 125
| 72 | New Jerusalem | 127
| 73 | Long Gone | 129
| 74 | God Speaks through Things | 131
| 75 | Freedom | 132
| 76 | Ennoblement | 134
| 77 | The Answer Is in the Thing Itself | 135
| 78 | Outside the Known World | 136
| 79 | Speak to Me of Higher Things | 138
| 80 | No Escape | 140
| 81 | Bittersweet | 142
| 82 | A Rarefied Atmosphere | 143
| 83 | A New Generation | 146
| 84 | Mythical Journey | 148
| 85 | Inglorious Descent | 150
| 86 | An Equivalence | 152
| 87 | Something to Think About | 154
| 88 | Identity | 156
| 89 | Conscience | 158
| 90 | God with Us | 159
| 91 | A New Dawn | 161
| 92 | Awake | 163
| 93 | Mutual Assent | 164
| 94 | A Jazz Band Somewhere in the Corner | 166
| 95 | American Dream | 169
| 96 | Maharishi | 171
| 97 | Mother | 173
| 98 | New Age | 174
| 99 | Intruder | 176
| 100 | Peace Be with You | 179
| 101 | With One Eye Open | 180
| 102 | A Window without Glass | 191
| 103 | A Vein to Paradise | 202
| 104 | Stating the Obvious | 209
| 105 | In Want of Evidence | 211
| 106 | Point of Departure | 213
| 107 | A Friend out of Nowhere | 215

1

Where I Belong

The flower's scent issuing from a cloud,
a mouth making movement
like a fish

starlight entering a cavern,
two stages of descent:

swirls of delight
impeded by an ache in the limbs,
a look of brethren
in pain,
a lick
from an animal disappearing into the undergrowth

hope pursuing termination in an answer.

2

Poetic Faith

The custodian who watched over the birth of memory
repeated what he had learnt
from the beginning:

"One love will fill the world,
one tongue voice approval for the right moment
to enter the teeming entity
you'll call 'home.'"

Divorced from paradise,
still replete
with a heart echoing through this millennium,
a pause before replying:

"No space wherein you do not abide,
no tree,
no flower, no ocean wherein you do not subsist

every blemish on our skin
the expanse
we'll divine your immediate presence."

3

The Outer Limit

Reed beds stood upright,
thunder resounded, a dove fluttered
in high winds

light reached the far wall, the blaze
opened the world to an eye

dust gathered in seams, milk dripped
to her calves

a pond leaked an odor
of spawn, the surface reflected the sky

an overlord subdued an animal kicking at his skull

drops splashed
from the moon, ancient mountains received the flow.

You'll value the transition
from a breast baked in clay
to zeal for your name scratched
in obsidian,
lift blocks until they reach the noonday sun,
launch an arrow
into the blue

blow pollen dust off buds into sleeplessness

drain fluid from the beast clamoring to eat you.

4

Mortal

Each bone
in its body will snap
when crushed against his chest,
moan in an ecstasy
of exhaustion,
struggle no more

be laid
by the way for all to ponder

it couldn't withstand the river
in flood, an even wider expanse
to reflect the light in the east,
fructifying power
in the skull, renewing vigor
to perform the feats
of epochs before he was born:

shadows long
as a body skewered
on a spit, ash
still aglow,
fat sizzling under chalcedony skies.

The sand
between his hands escapes his grasp,
drifts with an early morning wind

leaves tear with a beast seeking fledglings,
aimlessly flutter
on limbs underneath

blood thoroughly rinses after battle,
mingles with silica,
dull yellow
and salt

the pursuit of birds rising in ever widening circles
washes to the ground
in a downpour no one can withstand.

5

Hero

He can outrun anyone,
jump chasms with ease

escape the beast before it ensnares him

drive the wanderer from the moon's descent,
crush heads
with flint

defeat lesser mortals
who identify the secret
of longevity:

gore scraped from rods,
flesh drawn
from sacrificial victims

potency
in golden trinkets on the fingers.

6

All or Nothing

Ever present, you are there
when lids open
in cool winds anticipating return
to verdancy,
plump fingers scratch a baby's chin
and the date swells

like an open heart,
each blade of grass feels the warmth,
moisture evaporates,
leaving only dry veins and hot stubble

answers with fidelity returning to your firmament:

We belong
where glowing fields face the source
of light,
each drop rises toward an eye,
yet finds the sea with the same impulse
a lost lamb pricks up its ears
at the sound
of the flute echoing through the ranges:

"Let there be one."

7

At First Glance

In the inkling
of a lid fluttering upon soft flesh,
she startled. "Do I know him?"

To the core of her emphatically beating,
enigmatically entered,
joyful, pitying heart,
candor churned delight. "I love him."

As the flower between blue and yellow survived descent,
tributaries seeped to the lake
without shores,
the seraph minding the sun elevated an even brighter stellar cluster,
a ray reached into simplicity polarizing utterance
and heartache.

"I love her."

8

Earthbound

Align paths with circles surpassing a limited horizon,
orient evening's bleak landscape
with the glow sustaining earthly activity

through ether stained
with blood on the arc
spattered with mucus—

a child's,
newborn—

cast your glance beyond hoarfrost
and stubble pale as skin

for it is not warmth,
merely, which engenders the growth
of young shoots,
but memory of visitation

the definite stepping into constant concretion

the unmalleable sediment, "Us."

Stonehenge
Salisbury Plain
Wiltshire

9

Between the Earth and Cessation
of Carnal Imagery

Reaching out crops
stained by the insistence of lichen
to find imprints sustaining unicellular vitality,
escalloped
where inertia holds decline in agelessness . . .

wandering where radiance crackles
in unmoving potency,
melodies trill the bower

a breeze fans high plateaus,
a ray brightens the precipice,
the nova flares
through galaxies meeting no resistance . . .

apprehending pupil's increasing luster,
bursting
with no end point of concentration . . .

spinning pearl blue strands from limb
to limb,
awaiting reception
from the shore surpassing the cerulean expanse . . .

revealing the outrider's forehead with no words
to describe the height

(a rumble disappearing)

needled and violently bisected

in emission
from ruptured plenitude,
dripping nocturnal sap through skin,
bones and starless loss
of wakefulness hallucinating refrains,
"You belong,
stay where you are"—

a boneless daughter's mandible—

"I am yours,
you are mine,
you, I,
one only . . . "

encasing strata
crisscross scratched by zircon
and nickel,
uncovering the host teeming lime enriched droplets
and every inch caked with salt,
yet riddled with desire for regeneration . . .

spattering the immensity with beads,
condensing into stars
aglow with ejaculated ardor . . .

molding volcanic matter
with each foot regaining balance,
leaving ridges
and terrain scarred
by cheekbones . . .

mingling blood-stained tears
and the unstirred sea of saltless love

drops that never untouch,
displace or modify another.

Mootwingee
New South Wales

10

Aflame

All creaturely being has a focus:

the desire
to live.

All human intention
has a source:

scent
like rose,
one bud curled, reddish

an ant making its way
along a stalk,
gossamer traced with dew,
a will to continue
without faltering.

The solitary few have found a way
to follow
without losing contact
with the guide:

a twig
behind a leaf

a twig
before a shoot,
blue

between yellow

centered,
a twig behind a leaf

I am in the heart.

11

Sun God

When empty vessels clatter, gourds swirl
and tongues mimic ancients
on banks surrounding verdure,
can the blind spot encumbering the presence
of an all-seeing eye
be eradicated

heat
which can burnish stones,
damage fields, reduce a man
to dragging his feet in search
of relief?

Will subjects encounter a shadow
under lonely windpipes, coat eyelashes
with burnt twigs,
the leakage across powder congealing—

elucidate the bleeding body shimmering like waves
an inch above the stream,
elongate the worm that digs deeper
to avoid the glare
and the soft winged flight
exceeding the rays
burning it from beneath

fuse nescience
and air,
conquer realms of night

requite the countenance flattened against a pallid afternoon?

12

Afterlife

Naked you came into the world
where the descent transforming taste
and sight suspended
finds a flower resonating midday blue,
a jewel rays off the sea

an unblemished countenance
a message for your ears:

"With voluptuous gestures upheld
in reverence
you will conjure the same sureness writing in the heart
as the ineluctable fall
of an arrow,
the flow from your lids
as the river which feeds the desert
and the rain which motivates all plants to sprout

the pattern in bodily fluid
the stars on a balmy night.

As the great influx rises through your dreams
and the wash enriches a long harvest,
you will ride toward all you consider salubrious

the cord binding you

to misery

snap."

13

Over the Hill

A voice was heard:

Move on to the sun,
believe the lame are dying
and the sick need healing

believe
the adventure has only begun

you are free to go on alone,
depart before the moon passes
through the last shades of night

leave your honor intact.

A voice was heard:

Faithful to the lover
who needs protection,
I can extinguish the vagabond's yearning,
testify
to the demands of a pauper's hope,
direct a man to the heights
of prowess.

I long to diminish foreboding,
accept the inexhaustible pulling of your loins

nectar dispersed on ice

feel your mighty penetration.

I long to embody each strand
that runs through my fingers,
contort every muscle
with the fall to the earth

white clouds stirred
in slumber

give birth.

In your blood, numbing love
in the regret you'll hear
when you leave me.

14

Fingertips Seeking the Star's Goodwill

Curling leaves, carboniferous etchings

a turtle's back,
patterns
where incoming tides strive to penetrate substrates
of rock

salt infusing the lowest depths

eagles caught on crosswind,
white clouds resembling simple formations
on gutted clouds

inert,
unmoving droplets awaiting the first broken heart
to send them into freefall,
the spread
of blood
from a rainbow
to an egg

a mucus spattered child awakening in the sun.

Shadows creeping through twilight,
escarpments shifting to a point
that will settle and decompose on unsteady ground

vines enwrapping columnar pines,
a worm tasting soil under root

the unlived in hollow full of night

a moan tying charred skin to solar flares,
an underfed liver absorbing waves
that plump it full

bled raw glands holding back a tear,
a sliver
of light catching a corner of an eye

a pulse
in every hollow,
mountain and glade exactly positioned
where an otherworldly warrior answers
and reflects Orion's venal utterance.

                                                    Copake
                                        New York State

15

No Known End

"You who stand
at the foot of the world seeking enlightenment,
who understands movement deified in a speck of dust,
arrest the will
to become other than what is."

I arrive without name,
hold no illusions
to my sanctity

without purity,
a shadow,
a solitary voice.

"As you enter
swallow the pearl,
as you advance into the night
forsake your idea of what it means to be.
Surrender the trust you have
in eyes
which follow the sparkle on a river's descent
and ears that catch birdsong on a misty morning."

I cannot cross.

I am a warbler in the night,
a vocalist under the moon's aura

as I wait

stripped of entity

on thy border.

Valley of Pleistos
Greece

16

Arcadian Grace

As I brushed juice from your lips with my tongue,
nuzzled the vein protruding on your moistened nipple
and traced your carpals,
knees and lobes with a feather,
the vast arena turned in upon two hearts,
the pipes lulled us into slumber
and I heard the draught from the sea whispering fate:

"One like you is given to hear the moaning
of forgotten warriors,
the sobbing of untutored urchins
and the rasping of unlettered drunkards
who find release
in your capacity
to listen."

Corfu
Greece

17

A Long Way Down

Individuating your shining pate from the millions
who'll conceive more
than can be counted,
I caressed the skin stretching from ice caps
to the winged messenger's aural transcendence,
and breathed on your temple

an ambrosial wind ruffled your hair,
a bubble burst in the chamber prolonging vulnerability,
irises flared
in stellar smeared adulation

euphoric cycles returned and echoed,
millennia rushed in the void
while I sipped Bacchanalian nectar,
frozen wisps encircled our nexus
since I kissed your seamless mouth

sparsely punctuated verse substituted
for beads glistening on your uncovered torso.

A butchered calf

exquisite emissions
through lime tinted haze

ice,
loam and bedrock salt

undulation
on clean air turning inwards,
ferns imprinted in stone

reeds clotted with spawn,
the whirr of cricket's wings

caterpillars chewing leaves,
wet skin washed in lukewarm sea

blue

as the eye
of a God evading cold surrender
to a lonelier form,
numbed slowly

before descent into flesh.

Parthenon
Athens
Greece

18

Indivisible

Even if
the sanctuary of the God's reconfigures in brine
where a flower won't grow
and indigent lips wet the inner sun
and lasting memories imprinted
on its brilliance,
resilient characters will be preserved:

a maiden by the sea
and drops trickling down her spine,
the lift and lull
of her breasts
as she wades into the deep,
following,
smitten by her luxuriance

protected by the force
that borrows power
from libidinous ghosts behind each shadow,
descending where she
and I bind like seaweed around a rock,
a limpet holding fast to a stump,
a whelk in a shell tightly compacted

as the motion subsides.

19

Centaur

I'll not creep stealthily, but stamp my feet
on the rubble
as I pass.

I am not some insect
that shrilly declares its existence
from inside an abandoned shell, but a finely bred creature
who can expand his vison to include the horizon
as well as scrawls on parchment this side
and abandonment to treasures unlived in on the other.

I am not a tiny bird who finds it difficult
to ascend the heights beyond the clouds,
but a free-spirited traveler who,
in one leap,
can gain purchase on land that shimmers in the darkness,
takes millennia
to dissolve and leaves a remnant
sweet on lips which can say:

I have enlivened the sea with light,
nullified the encroachment of saturnine interlocutors
who'll question my imperative
to transcend the limit placed on flesh
and matter,
since I must abide
by the fruition demanded by my descendants
who must spring into life

unbeknownst
to under dwellers,
live in the presence
of one who loves me.

20

Fruit

The blood
on your calf is from a wound sustained in battle
with an enemy who desired to eradicate the idea
you remembered
where you were from, pale flowers
in the wreath at your feet
from the same tree I saw in a dream
quivered in an idyllic wind and fell
when no one was looking,
the cup
in your hand contains the nectar
all should drink

it brings vitality to the joints,
health to the muscles
and belongs to the witness
who can watch all things embody
and gel:

the tissue
between your fingers spread
when you related
how dry
the heels pushing into grey soil,
coarse the skin losing moisture under an intense noon,
brittle the ligaments
when frost coating every plane upturned
and bare patch hiding in shadow
felt warm against dying pith,
gnarled an olive on the mountainside

at its roots,
a witness to outgrowth, an immanent voice
so definite
it cannot but be heard
in silence:

molded to withstand pain
a bone gives structure to ascent,
a sure footed stance
ensures the extremities mingle with hot air
and bring it to settle in blindness

a mortal knows fear of expiration in summer heat,
accepts the last act
of obedience to nothingness
and values its own achievement.

21

Mortification

No one can outperform my capacity
to take hold of things
and bend them into a shape
which befits the body I walk and sleep in,
vivify the health
of every mortal atrophying in the pallor
of lunar scarcity
without the blaze at noon warming the marrow

pursed lips:

the taciturn mastery which forbids the weed
to blossom in the shadows

a furrowed brow:

thought engaging with the hierarchies

luminous eyes:

clarity
to see the many when they fall,
the few when they rise

a hollow between left
and right starved of fluid:

an insect waiting for rain to fill its abdomen
with life

frozen liver:

a mole
with ragged edges
on a white back

green tubes:

burnt matter spiraling to a stain free atmosphere

a bruised tendon:

the tempest's attempt
to bring noise
and fury
into self-satisfaction swirling to the ground.

22

Awakening

Scalloped in a bleeding shell,
knowing how long the trial has been,
yet unaware
of how to push outwards
and partake of freedom
in the nebulous sky

molded for a lifetime, reviling the force
which holds down all attempts
to seek another plane beyond mortal failure

constrained in a world
that knows no outlet,
pleading for the means to transform corporeality
with no end, or the coursing
of vital fluid through embodiment,
into motion in accordance
with light upon a fingernail
and a palm frond stretching further than the blue.

23

Heritage

You,
who would dissuade the movement away from love
to despair in self-full self-reflection,
empowered to enter the marrow of suffering
and the texture of loneliness calling for self-forgetfulness,
a solitary figure traversing the wasteland,
distance punctuated by screams of the lost,
are entrusted to wash clean self-doubt,
the inability to face the higher always

to presume deliverance foreshadowing unsullied existence,
but never one
like mine

crafted from turgid milk
and fetal residue,
fashioned out of matted hair and dribble,
spliced with gorilla bone

and lying into the mirror.

24

Revival

No enemies devour the treasure
or substitute worship
of the past
for the present sense of ever-present identity

the abeyance of doubt.

I am not the ground as it disappears in a windstorm,
nor pain coursing the desert
which never perceives an end
to its expanse—

one empty sky,
rock
and defiles—

but the resumption of a heartbeat
when soil has covered every pore
and blood stagnated a forgotten pool beneath an outcrop,
joy illuminated
by a vast presence transcending each
and every muscle,
bone
and ligament

equal only
to two
or three words spoken in the darkness:

"Step
out of your shell

I love you."

25

VIRTUAL DEATH

Even though
we hang him to crudely sawn lengths of wood
he still forgives,
even though the faithful call on him
to remain in this stream we call life,
he is behooved,
and against passion to answer supplication,
to slip under the weight of natural tendency
to congeal upon the earth

as his identity is stronger than the Antagonist's need
to suffocate the imperfectly contoured essence
in every heart

be it now,
then
or ever

as long as he descends to infuse the dust
with white hot veracity,
incurs the scythe,
bones floating upward

the beast clawing another mucus spattered face
into an effigy of abandonment

yet,
unknown to the few

whom he trusted to join on the path
beside the heaving waters and rock-strewn fields,
indubitably,
as the turning wheel hasn't crushed his Father's seed
into characterless pulp

alive.

26

Pieta

She longed to pluck him
like an insect from a web,
place him between her flanks

protect him from the challenge
that would desecrate love,
acquit him from the need
to follow his calling,
overcome the act
he is entwined within.

She
must embrace a corpse streaked with blood,
punctured by thorn,
emptied of light through forlorn eyes

accept a caricature,
weep over the flesh
we believed
would return to sanctuary beyond persecution
molded in drops of concupiscence
and offal thrown to a malfeasant dog's need to eat,
alter the inevitable flow

revive a living well in the body
which descended to teach the meaning
of sacrifice
and mutually bound concomitance
with motherhood

27

A Personal Inclination

I would walk the path of reverence
until the storm has subsided
and melts with an absence
of friction

this is my way.

Mine is to raise intelligence beyond suffering,
overarch ignorance with the verity of insight.

I will rend darkness,
shatter obstinacy,
echo the command
to dispense with evil.

My wont is to select jewelry
from a precious vein,
train my eye on the play of color
and avoid hearing the task I could accomplish
if,
for a moment of clarity
I turned
and accepted higher calling.

All have individual sensitivity,
each his consistent manner,
but together unravel the Word, cancel doubt,
the abandonment of holy might

restore faith,
offering aspiration like stars
of indefinite magnitude evinced through compassion
where the turning wheel has stopped
on the outskirts
of paradise.

28

Gnosis

Slay me,
and bury me in supernal climes,
leave an epitaph scribbled extemporaneously.

With broken nails I traversed the ice floe,
reached the summit, and gave no thought
to the mechanisms of a turning wheel.
As the valley smoldered,
I ate of the oak,
planted my feet on the outcrop,
and recited epistles teeming with light.

My force is a sentence
and a word struck with veracity,
my provenance the final stanza
of a million themes protected from the razor's sweep.
I have lengthened the motif, and returned it with gratitude.

When moisture steams into billowing clouds,
I will solidify
into a droplet

when heat dissipates on withering fingertips,
you'll star fleck my interior
until it burns

when the green outgrowth droops from lack of rain,
I will,
in morning splendor,
face your countenance.

29

HIGH PRIESTESS

With the sun between my eyes
I could see
into worm addled skulls
and blind them

stars in my feet,
pass over their gluttonous advance,
rise higher beyond the ether that enlivens them
and douche it

sap in my blood,
stick feet to heather
and bones to withering grass.

My veins filter through the undergrowth,
pores secrete bright fluid
filling a flower cup

my womb breeds progeny out of leaves curling,
raindrops pattering
and sighs accompanying the breeze over fields.

30

At Home

Elsewhere than nexus with turmoil
or intentions reaching luminously
to the heights with an aura
of success
dreams congeal in sublimity:

free of the demand
for movement in the limbs
toward your brother in arms
dribbling from a fractured jaw,
or the cloying pungency
of your wife giving birth
to a son who will share your interests
and pursue a course
that may bring wisdom and honor
like prophets resonating the law,
staining the sky with new promise,
you will be addressed by messengers
in vestments spun from starlight,
who inhabit realms beyond personal desire
to stand securely
without falling:

the prosaic enriched by rhythms sensing the end
is a beginning

the old renewed
without the loss
of what makes it sense its own place.

31

Guardian of Forgotten Kingdoms

I sustain the verdict:

Guilty!

prolong the accusation:

Wrongdoing!

have no qualms in levelling the sword
at your belly, placing my finger
into the scarlet mist saturating the onlooker.

The sentient universe will feel my pulse
and swallow tears of rain,
for I commune outside human destiny
directly with the hierarchy ordering me
to consummate Jupiter's passion tapering to my skull
and, in league with untutored minstrels
who play
as if smitten by a Goddess's charm
as she combs her hair
in silver morns spread from earth
to the zenith,
to raise my voice until the sun fails,
the moon falls
and every sentence written on the stars
and planetary bodies echoing a past
that made them is granted to be mine or,

at least, secured in the wonderment
I divined when I looked upon my image
in burnished metal

to dominate
until the new ruler pronounces my guilt,
submit
to his deliverance:

REX

You are our witness.

Align the cosmos.

Goddess

As a whisper haunts the cell
of a captive,
"You will be free when you give unto the state
your body and aspiration,"
I will render victory
over Hades inhabited by denizens
who know no avenue from its defiles.

If the sun shines
on a statue's tresses frozen
by light having left the mood
that conjures taste in entia
with ardor,
I'll illumine the pressure to mold my lobe
and irradiate the texture of meandering in shadows
below my abode.

When ice refreshes an assistant
on a dusty platform,
I'll caress each brow
with a kiss
not of an isolated pass
tender in execution.

As an entity proceeds to breathe
in the pearl white skull,
you will inhale rarefied air
and sup the tears I have shed
for your indignity
in flesh and cartilage.

33

Enrichment

Each seed that sprouts
and each tendril that reaches the air
has been made with a promise:

the fructification of human endeavor
will have the same quality
as nectar ripening in autumn,
the fulfilment of a youngster growing to maturity
dependent
on the ground in which it is prepared

trust:

organic matter building the soil

love from a lucidly beating heart:

water
which fills the runnels
and flows to an all absorbing root

the Word resounding in your quick,
"I love you:"

the gardener tending with forethought
and interest
the patch he'll cultivate
and nurture.

34

Deliverance

When the Holy Name is uttered
by the well
or in the street, you will be challenged
and expected to give allegiance
to a pagan
who worships his shadow
and gods disappearing in ether.

You will be asked to submit, kiss his ring,
realize his consequence above all man.

You will perplex him with denial,
estrange him with contrition:

Can a cure be sought
in the vials strewn before his munificence,
would his retinue bound to follow on all fours
call me over the bodies maimed at his command
to live on leaving my shadow
by the cold stream?

I am lonely,
it isn't possible
to be more lonely, desperately afraid
of his insignia pounded indelibly to the coal face,
his demonic blue eyes that swallow my own.

How can I continue
where his drive reeks of self?

I can't.

"I will be with you
and divulge my secret:

"Incomplete without you,
I love you."

35

A Detached Point of View

Although I am
from Heaven and penetrate earthly deeds,
you'll believe I'm lost in the clouds

value the insights of bearded men
than light surrounding devotion,
wound the rhythm in reluctance
to trust

a trace from another world

each time the earth is tilled,
and worms can be seen wiggling,
suffocating from abundance
of air, and damp penetrates your skin, doubt
the descent has reached this far
and question
who lives in the soil:

Silent trusting
Archangels above
in perfect listening,
calling,
"OM LISS JOY,"
simple annunciation:

"Now we are true,
enamored above

we'll course the shadows
and flecks of malignity
where the child
has lost its finger
in the snow,
bypass an irregular heartbeat

follow the path through the maze
of human dissent,
revitalize water in the womb

inspire the will
to remain kneeling,
the sun to show its countenance,
the moon to reflect its glory

the force of veneration
that dwells in each soul
express love.

The Philosopher.

36

To the Far Ends of the Earth

The dandelion
on the lea has been trodden on
by a donkey,
the rose in the lane
eaten by a goat,
the lily under the oak squashed by a herd
and the immortal power that grows in tissue
silenced in concupiscence.

What caught
his vital fluids?

Did they flow and stain the vessel,
or rinse immediately
on touching the heaviness of our making?

Would markings provide a clue
to his whereabouts?

Could dregs,
the fact of evidence,
remain to confound the skeptic,
who disbelieves
but who'll recast doubt
in the probability a mouth tasted wine,
a nose breathed the aroma of fermentation,
a heart sensed the flow from vein to vine,
root to spring,
membrane to tendril?

We must find the object
and restore it to the high point.

Not just an icon wrought in metal symbolizing the transference
between this world and another,
the messenger announcing the turning point
to the gates of New Jerusalem,
but unborn substance mingling with ichor
and tears from an abode
mindful
of suffering in the womb.

We should hold it aloft,
so the world can contemplate incorruptibly.

Not only the aura meeting darkness in the temple,
the indefinite light following the design
meant for utility and function,
but valor spread to the elements peeling back
from the silent end
and ardor fed
between the halves breaking into day
and night

a flower erect in the field.

37

Mission

The sea flows
between healthy rule committed to invigorating the spirit
in confusion
and druids
who forsake homilies witnessed beyond outer boundaries:

veins in my hand
blue
with cold
run with the fire of conviction.

The waves rise and fall
between clarity imparted to a follower
who bows before the candle
on a frosty morning
and mounds entombing the answer
to travail:

the netherworld brings forth inclement nights
on the path of denial.

Thunderclouds separate orisons
devoted to one
who fills recondite graves with light
and eyes blanched with salt:

lamb's blood will drench cracked heels,
wash black marks
and rinse nodules spent of fluid
when the heavens open.

The storm on the horizon recedes into coves,
birdlife attempt awkward spirals
in heavy rain deafening calls
for release

the mixture of presentiment
and well water overflows:

allow the glow appearing over the shoals
to emanate in new intensity,
unfurl the sail
in a wind born of higher resolve,
cross the expanse
with the speed of an angel
to broken inlets
and islets

forthwith.

Bangor
Northern Ireland

38

The Great Architect

After you have removed the monuments
of an empire
you will have my statement:

Not the intricacies of law
but the expanse of justice.

Not the inert plates
of mortal form
but a swollen heart
and the intention
to encapsulate freedom
in light transcending the lowliness
of human affliction.

Not the exegesis of ancient text ministered
through parchment and candlelight
but the mark of the Servant
who identifies space
with obedience and each hour
with forgiveness.

Identify
as the instrument guiding the hand sketching every line.

Construct each portion as if the whole
were dependent on them to stand.

Mortise them as if the blood
and sweat
of the divine Arche
were the substance you work with.

For you do not claim responsibility
or ownership

you are coeval with the Creator
in execution only
and the glorious Idea that springs anew
each instant you turn to the Heavens
is his alone.

                                                          Hagia Sophia
                                                         Constantinople

39

Beneath the Cross

Burnished
with sunlight, rubbed
with loving fingers, corroded
with salt, open
to the elements
and the moods
of passers-by:

tension— holy visitants contemplating the Word

mystery, revelation, joy—

the inert quickened
to vitality.

Witness
to undying transformation:

blood and flesh
into a gaze that penetrates each moving part,
slumber into an acre sown
in tenderness

indigo hills, leaves of flame,
gold columns and ice.

Born in the days when Adam tasted a raindrop
on Eve's forehead,
alive when the woman
with stars on her brow
knew the pains of labor

replete
in a cloud anticipating downfall,
uncapturable
like thistledown
in a gale hurrying to the moon

immanent
in mud saturated with bodily fluid,
concentrated
as an eye following return
to the heart's rest

reverence, plainsong

intermittent breath, self-denial

insignia drawn
in a wound reopening at sunset,
gathering stones to embody each line

muscles strained, hands grazed,
placing a rock on top

witness to the hierarchies,
abode
of the gentle

maker of vision.

                                                    Iona
                                                Scotland

40

Tranquility

The mist on the lake:

the breath
of a dragon descending from the clouds
bent on discovering why pavilions stretch beneath
and eager eyes look up,
on the lookout
for his approach.

The shimmer of light
on the water:

the reflection
from an emboldened eye casting its glance
toward a serene gaze into the flare,
with the hope of catching sight
of the birth
of desire
to see all
it can see.

The pink lotus opening to its full extent:

a fresh heart accompanying another
in the downward spiral into flesh.

West Lake
Hangzhou

41

ART IS ITS OWN REWARD

Past midnight
the candle is flickering,
veins of blue,
ovals of yellow reappear,
blur and merge

eyesight is failing me I am sure.

An owl hoots,
the boy who brings a morsel is asleep
in a corner,
the ghost of the aged caretaker
who burnt coals
for our numbed feet has ceased
to sigh.

Now
to the text:

each line will combine with meaning,
flow to supersede affliction impounding action
and substitute the beneficent will determined
before the advent of disquiet.

Each dot,
point and crossed letter
will assume greater proportion
when viewed by a prince
or a king

(the Emperor already has ordered a copy)

an honor for an unworthy such as myself
who'll take another fresh page,
articulate with candor
and precision
the very Name
of Scripture that signifies achievement

present it
unto one
who values it above all things.

42

Pilgrim

Who
did I encounter
on the path this morning:

an old traveler carrying sticks on his back,
burdened
with the daily task
of having to provide food and warmth

his feet stained from blood oozing from cracks

a monk, with a breviary
in his satchel,
reciting the prayers learnt from childhood

each syllable stressed with each pulse,
each vowel declaring loneliness,
sympathy and devotion
will bring him closer to the tomb
of one who breathed in the presence
of the higher
than earthly, motivating self-sacrifice

a kind-hearted fellow who nominated a passage
for the way
beneath the boughs stippled
with lichen:

clandestine light, brushing wings

noble burn forsaking knowledge
for love,
paring the sensual
from dreams—

wasted gruel coating a pot—

venerating,
in malady,
the witness who follows every step?

43

Pillage

Ancestral voices murmur in every cell:

"We belong to one race issuing an imperative
in tissue and lymph,
a cry
in malleable cultures sweating infertile gel,
an ageless song:

We will return
and bear witness:

No one will withstand the prow
in unexplored oceans,
nourishment in negation, matter disintegrating
and violence preceding peace

entanglement
in elemental intensity,
concretion awaiting exhumation
of spring

the hammer smashing your skull."

Store Baelt
Denmark

44

Alms

Visitors have finished prayer and file toward the exit.

Look at archway
upon archway
and wait for a shadow
to appear between the columns.

You cannot see a face
or elicit sense from conversation.

Possibly one is wearing clothes
of the finest quality
perfumed like wildflower amongst rock
and scrub
on the hillside,
white as cream.

You have no hand to push the plate forward
or foot
for support
against the cornerstone.

Start your chant,
ask the deepest question:

"Do you mean to follow
in the footsteps of the praised one?

Then place a coin before my recumbent figure."

            Great Mosque
              Cordoba

45

Grey Stone Winter

With your return you'll want feet
to stand securely upon solid ground,
eyes
to peer into the furnace and hands
to erect a dwelling place existing for centuries.

The space between the walls
will belong to one who transcends the dire route
of misapprehension— the Lord,
the air in the dungeon inhaled by one occupant—
the evil doer,
grit
in the battlements sourced from one plane—
the earth,
the gate at the entrance hoisted for one reason—

protection.

Lincoln Castle
England

46

A Glorious Enterprise

Blue— the true believer.

Red—
the warrior who'll outwit the Antichrist.

White—
the star guiding a lonely monk
who fathomed his dreams
for a baby born
to be kissed or,
at least, its shadow lingering on upswept stables
where a bone
or stalk may be found.

Black— night enveloping a son's helmet
discarded alongside its owner
and a weeping mother
who'll never silence the bubbling beneath her knees.

Regard the vestige
of the throne you sought to erect
where rose tinted evenings cross over
and acclaim dawn's scattered tinctures,
asseverating naught
that contumely could divulge—

the mixture
of generosity and submission
fired to the point of fluidity transcending fear
ground in obscurity.

Motionless air allowing easier access
to our hearts, a spire touching the lower reaches
of your condescension
to visit

a buttress upholding the attempt
to reinstate incorruptibly in Spring,
a stained-glass window, as lambent hues fall
on an upturned forehead,
empowering your minion who'll vow the return
of the Savior

to this plane.

Cathedral Notre Dame
Chartres
France

47

Soon to Be Free

What I hoped for
when I knelt before the altar
that I believe is,
was and always will be,
a calling to trust the light
which has vanished somewhere beyond,
must be articulated
in order to fulfil innermost desire
to accord with meaningful nature.

There is nothing
that can't be discerned behind the fear.

The desire to realize your passion,
a tender wound
in shadow light,
surrendering to the unknown,
"We cannot take it without you,"
can be read as:

Like blood spattered on a white wrist,
I'll stand out from the contours of the earth

my heartbeat will resound,
eyes reflect distant rays
and my limbs,
denuded of movement,
will be the space you'll implant your impulse

there are creatures which survive
even though their feet
are mangled, birds that flap loosely
even though their wings are clipped,
a silent breast that feels warmth
even though the origin
of fire hides behind a blanket of smoke.

No one who deems the broken tryst reparable
can discover the meaning
of holy otherness
unless he raises into the furnace
and reconstructs devotion
with a question,
"How can insight into your nature
be maintained?"

"Return to us,
oh Lord, return,
lest we fall foul to the evil influence,"
can be reconfigured:

We know your nature.

You are the great mover,
redeemer
and ontological sustainer of our very quick.

There is reason to know what has gone
will come back,
what has risen will descend,
what has become motionless,
unsighted and inert will,

by the law
of an opposite succeeding its opposite

proceed into our hearts.

The Dom
Cologne

48

A Lute Player's Homage

Perhaps a melody to erase the consternation
or an arpeggio to heal the wound
sustained from warfare with the Evil One.

You are in no mood
for the crashing of worlds destroyed in the maelstrom,
nor prepared to endure formations manifesting taste
impervious to the issue from the wellspring.

Rather, leagues
from a mendicant fondling a moth longing for flurry
enamored with the light-hearted
and transitory, you would prefer the exact chord
resonant
with a mountain bird's call

the flow of lifeblood
from a martyr's unerring faith,
the immanent tone reflected through blistering rose

extraordinarily nimble and euphonically coherent emanation.

Chartres
France

49

Betrothal

With the accompaniment of choirs,
trumpets
and minstrels,
shower petals over the foam tossed sea

offer the orb incarnating the distillation
of chastity,
douche wine where lips touch

usher in the profoundest of respect,
as passion drifts with folly from the interior
wherein the darkest secret steeps addiction
to festive gaiety with a portent:

only two can join as one,
no other share in union sanctified by the author
of human existence.

The flame between the soul
and center will cross
and light the candle waiting to receive illumination,
the well shed its stream
yet dam the flow pouring from the other's breast,
replenishing joy lost
in the other's heart

the abyss buried in the sarcophagus,
all but one will eschew,
render the secret of identity
unto the other

replace disquiet in the mortal losing silence
unto she who will be his wife,
unto he
who will be her husband.

50

Release

I haven't time to savor unworldly vision,
nor to cherish wisdom,
yet I claim victory
for the luminary over the agents
of desecration
who expected to extinguish the lamp
and spill its oil—

fomented sheen
on blood,
unstirred like the tomb's odor, coarse
like a stallion chewing grass—

and wait for the hoarfrost to settle.

Vigilant,
I have remained

in death long no more
for another word.

51

From the Diary of Brother Simon

Ambrose called me across the cloisters,
bade me see him.

Judgement:

"Brother Simon, I have a lump under my arm.
Is it dangerous?"

I carve a name on a timber found near the well.

Midnight Chimes:

numbed by solitude,
softened by acceptance,
I dig closer toward the sycamore tree,
loosening sod
with a twist,
depositing it in line with the grave

closer to where the universe contracts
to give birth before return to far flung perimeters.

Ambrose must be buried.

Grace:

when the night has finally lost denial
of luminance and cheer,
I will settle by the arbor,
anticipate love
will reach me,
even though
my bones fed marrow
to limbs delighting in shameful deeds
and my tongue lisped words
of hatred
when the juvenile who licked the throats
of mercenaries brought in to protect the few
from folly would have been better off dead.

I tend to trees in the orchard.

Manna:

a cherry splits open,
droplets splash
on my wrist

a stain
the shape of planetary bodies
encircling a cherub
dissolves
as I lick gingerly.

I bandage the cut
received while honing blades.

Omega:

sparrows lay eggs on the rafters,
a kitten mews under the floorboards

a spider sinks into a corner,
the afternoon sun,
obscured once
by blossoming nebulae,
streams forth
and lights the courtyard

jars raise irregular shadows, the bush I tend
for culinary flavor acquires a momentary gloss.

I alone have the key
to unlock the outer door

a passing child may notice the monotonous click.

Gloucester Abbey
England

A Word for All

I'll list my grievances
beside your flower beds

make sure you see them,
read them
and ponder upon them:

the lad in the stable
must not be avoided
when he asks to see a letter in the Scriptures,
the virgin shall be allowed
to attend mass when she wills

the saint in his alcove,
when the blessed ghost appends its dictates
to the fact
all must share equally
in the divine afflatus,
bring it to hand
in the darkest of inks.

53

THE GRASS, THE TREES, AND RIVERS

The unsqualled ocean
neither in nor out there . . .

all possible futures counterpointing the elevation
of atomistic intensities to undistorted spheres . . .

the enigmatic distillation
solidifying into an earthbound mold
uncomplicated by illusions
of life immaterial.

Golden Buddha
Bangkok
Thailand

54

A New Order is Formed in the Temple

When the sun fades, the moon's aureole denied
in the night's spoliation,
a cry will come up from the cloth:

"The ventricle burst,
cupped fingers received the flow."

A receptacle
to sip the nectar clear as Spring:

the impulse to disengage a wayfarer
bound for verdant fields
and humus rich soil
because he hasn't learnt
how to address the gods
must be forsaken.

A maudlin keeper rinsed from head to foot
opening the doors throughout the maze:

the tessellated face
staring toward a blue lizard
escaping through dead wood,
the Babelic drone caught
in the instant a fly lands in glue

the incision
in a mentor's heart
leaving him to join the pieces,
the transparent orb
just out of reach
of fingertips probing the equally see-through expanse
on the other side of a dragon's mouth.

A white robe to join the few
who sing as if each word
has the power
to heal:

a dead man's zest
lit up by the flame
on the altar receding into a warrior's veins
and blossoming like an early variety
of summer rose
on his abdomen
shaped like a cross.

55

The Doge Recognizes a New Form of Entertainment

He struggles
with what he knows not

I   poised at the threshold
       ready to transform and liberate

II   her dominion, surrendering self will

III   intimately conscious,
       devoted
       to seeking the Word,
       following without hindrance

IV   with the greatest power,
       immense effort, massive intention

V   rendering unto Heaven the smallest detail,
       sacrificing for Eternity
       the World

VI   embracing union
       and not the one who,
       in rapture,
       finds inertia
       in light
       and emptiness in volition

VII   forward,
controlling the direction,
willfully returning,
and onward

VIII   to deem the accurate,
impartial decision in the conscience
which has extricated from the demand for justice

IX   without relinquishing one step,
illuminating obstacles encountered
in the heart

X   where fate
is often less reluctant
to suffer the perils of an unknown source
than to accept the deeper yearning,
the longing of an earthly creature
to make sense
of tribulation

XI   constraining lesser ramblings
and pleasures,
up righting the overturned chalice,
replenishing a fiery liquid:

XII   an imperative
to realize ultimate deliverance
is dependent on the will
to overturn dogma, face the flow
from uninterrupted silence
and breathe in the remote atmosphere
far from prescription

XIII   where order has begun to decay
       in the macabre dance preceding annihilation,
       fearful rhythms preceding abandonment in isolation

XIV   in balance
       between forces,
       without one trying to outdo the other

XV   accepting the mind rests within the bones
       where serpents lie,
       again and again . . .

XVI   moving with an elemental cycle
       toward blossoming,
       falling like a stone fruit
       stripped of skin
       and destination . . .

XVII   an uncommon luminance
       where night meets its opposite descrying a pattern
       having no bound
       or termination . . .

XVIII a softer luminance evincing the shadow
       where bane and grief pull the innocent
       toward the chamber concealing the lonely angel
       who soothes over the ungracious impulse . . .

XIX   reinvigorated
       as an answer to ungodly acts
       that have no apparent cause,
       transforming the quest
       to light up hidden defilements . . .

XX   anointing the body from realms
      beyond sense immobilized
      in an aura enamored with an ageless Word,
      the explicit judgement:

XXI   The Kingdom of Heaven is within
      and will be listened for
      in the profoundest
      and simplest of human activities.

                                    The Tarot—Major Arcana
                                                     Venice
                                                      Italy

56

Masterpiece

Until the age
is consummated in the balance of the earthly
with patterns motivated
by halcyon presentiment,
I shouldn't presume
to have found the point
where the star drawing nearer
to incarnation in bone
has re-entered a common principality,
eyes reflecting light from an artisan's workbench

the same intensity that guided the Magi.

A vein following a hero toward apotheosis,
a scapula molded
to presage the advent of contours flowing in a world
without sorrow,
framed in a heart
separated from fear of failure

a broken hand healed
by rhythm, a fingernail completed
with patience

an ancient deity
in marble
transfigured
by a maker who seeks no comfort
in anonymity.

Angel

I will not condemn plans
to erect statues reaching the acme
of artistic realization,
however
I am beyond reproduction

the night vague
then lucid, the dream clear
then tainted with doubt

my aura present then far away.

I have left a trace,
an inkling of my calling:

the countenance
you seek,
the hardly discernible substance you aspire to

the fleeting,
otherworldly nuance suggesting the end
of division and anxiety

still appears

on the outskirts

of sanity.

58

Profundity

A merchant has arrived with goods
from another region quite unlike those
we produce here.
He has stuffed his pockets with fruit
and gorged himself on wine.

A priest has come by to counsel rulers,
our magisterial makers
who,
in planning the city precincts
to include a comfortable path for the sinner,
have realized
if they are to spend an eternity
in suffering
then best to spend hope
in a denial of as much pain as they can.

A traveler from the north
accompanied by a lady friend
is visiting a chapel,
no doubt impressed
by our capacity to deliver the grandeur
of the ancients
in the intimate interior
beloved of the proponents of articulate rhythms.

A scholar has retreated to an alcove,
thankful he has light to study by,
a Script
to illuminate others

a master of rhetoric,
notary
to the principles of judgement,
an advisor
to the ignorant,
a specialist to the learned.

After midnight, he'll be in seclusion,
fathoming disavowal of having arrived
where the Word means
exactly what he wants it to mean

for just beyond
is another word
in the absence
he can only just reach

in silence.

59

Work of Art

No one can substitute flesh with ink or gristle
with pigment nor can bones be crushed
with water
and oil
to reproduce their curves
and indentations,
an eyeball is unable to fathom its interior
and enhance the absence
with luster on velvet black,
the nipple is beyond execution,
the mole beyond practice

a voice will never speak from the canvas
or the toenail scrape the earth accidentally,
the bramble never puncture your skin
as on the day of His indignity
or the temple be reached
by a lonesome traveler
on a journey

the bud will,
however,
appear to glisten
with dew—

an unearthly patina surrounding her pail
as she gathers water—

the cuckoo extend its beak as if transfixed
in a call obeying songs from the deity,
her face radiate hope
in having heard softly from the heights,
"I love you,"
the light streaming through the clouds,
so alike to the landscape
from my window,
reveal behind the thistle,
rock and child playing with a broken urn,
the gentle will
of He who would create a less than perfect realm
in His likeness.

60

Now to Work

I have sketched horned beasts
and impoverished children,
smeared fragrant oil
on a eunuch slumbering in a doorway
and the sweat
of a wrestler in the arms of an adversary,
but never learnt to mix Heaven's brew
with ointment
from a sinner blessed by the saints.

I have concentrated
on flagellants in pain
and the brusque step of a warrior
on his way to battle, shaped a body
in indolence
and a skull brittle
as eggshell,
but haven't defined a matron's breast
nor opened her eyes
behind their gaze of loneliness.

My name isn't Jesus
or Lucifer
nor will it be sustained in perpetuity,
my abode neither angelic
or preternatural,
but every stroke is the execution
of my own vision
for I am too lazy to keep it up.

I relinquish, therefore,
a claim to greatness,
because in my most lucid glance
into the haze rising from a road,
can never penetrate its essence
or,
when evocative and entrusting its secret,
can't be bothered to raise it
with a love of oaths
anointed in wine and myrrh

but, whatever I produce
can be deemed sacred,
because I am made
in the likeness
of He
who is subject to a promise:

"There are moments intensified
in my gift

enhanced
by my unfailing delight
in what you have done."

61

Luminous Night

The church bell tolled once for my sweetheart
in finery,
twice for the moon above,
thrice for the nectar of love

I am incomplete
without you,
an instant forgotten,
a note abandoned

I am alone
without you,
apart from your unearthly luminance
I am at a loss
for guidance

I will discern pinecones
and needles on banks white with snow,
trace footprints with a feather

call on you to accompany me.

62

Blessed Release

We are forsaken, we grieve,
we suffer waiting for an envoy
to expel the demonic power,
reinstate sobriety
and thinking incarnate

lest we forget,
we are obliged to reconstruct the New Temple
of Jerusalem in stone

burnished to reflect the ray streaming from Heaven,
sculpted
to follow the aspiration
from the image within, engraved
with the Word
to disclose the will enabling all things
to take place,
painted on
to transmute the dance hidden
in the breast touched with the glory
into an expanse
even a lowly penitent is able to pray under

in silence trusting ascension,
below accepting revival,
at the center evoking the contours
and specifications of masters
who created edifices
that still defy the elements
retaining proportions echoing down the centuries:

mass and spatial symmetry in perfect unity,
line
and plane integrated in harmony

whose intention and execution show,
with grace
no less than love realizing the function
of the Creative,
vigilantly valuing submission
and death,
a trace in bottomless need

resonance lifting harm
into clarity, matter
into substance, darkness into life.

                                                        St Peter's
                                                       Vatican City

63

Heliocentric

A day isn't bound around the point of feeling
nor dependent on a birth
to sustain it.
An interior doesn't yearn
for its likeness in blood
nor does the moon require sensitivity
to engender visibility.
The motion
of the stars
isn't subject to delight
nor do rainbows submit to the cause of freedom.
The limpet doesn't cling to a wreck
because it fears the inevitability
of decay
nor is it necessary for a bone
to be analyzed
known before eaten by a hungry dog.

What we desire
as important in the sight of a creator
isn't necessarily what happens
in the mind of the divine.

Where we belong
isn't determined
by a center made in our image
nor do we need to clamor for superiority.

We are at the edge
and can see into the inferno
as it absorbs the will
of He who is all light.

64

A Humanist's Aspiration

I am not raising into the Spirit
if it means substituting glass and stone
for an untouchable heavenliness
that could neither be hoped to be lived in or,
even if the Savior is faithful
to His word to empty corrupted aisles
that hold us for centuries,
accommodate longing to be with Him
where He may assume awesome indescribability
beyond speculation

His abode ablaze
is not ours to furnish
with mistakes, ineptitude
in consequence of action
in penury
must finger the cuts as they bleed,
feel the sweat on cheeks,
taste saliva, grind the seed for bread

our rooms must shelter us,
our beds support us
and our eyes apprehend the greatness
of achievement
if we are to believe
we have the potential to rise
at last worthy of His name.

Chateau Chambord
France

65

An Artist's Tool

A brush stroke like a wounded gull
swooping to an early morning drizzle,
and between absence of form
and the gaze from a nearly open iris,
a twist and turn catching light
in an old eye

a smudge in advance
of three lines
directed out of pith, the shudder
that contains itself in the rush toward the earth,
and the severed trunk spouting immortal liquor.

The impetus
to copy the markings
that belong to the actual body standing before me—

the life reminding me
I, too, once twittered,
sang
and was shot at—

and a feather plucked by a stained hand
to serve as the instrument
of a purpose
fine as flight.

Tokyo
Japan

66

Fruits of the Spirit

The wonder isn't
that I hear tones betokening the advent
of your love and glory
as you bless the very stuff I carry within me,
but that my neighbor hasn't fathomed the profundity
of your visitation

sooner
or later
it must be accepted
as God breathes in all creatures.

The mortal
must inevitably die, decay
and be eaten by worms,
yet as the darkness surrounds on all sides
he may see a light leading upwards unbound

no dream believes itself
in another world which speaks with authority,
"You have arrived."

The blessing really is to acknowledge
although I disrupt the cause
of goodwill with anger, malice
and impetuosity,
the temper of a child
who is still discovering his bodily functions,
a quiet voice will penetrate to my knees,
"I love you"

no meaning,
no text,
no word disclosed by believers,
devoted as they may be
to the power of the Spirit,
can substitute their revelation for the resounding impression
uttered with conviction, "I am".

67

OUT OF REACH

My heart could not have asked for more that night
Than seas of storm and broken, pallid moon;
Mortal strings of youth beside the firelight
And dewy lids upon the pillow down,
Notes astounding long forgotten shepherds
Bypassing thrones known only to regents
And settling in my breast, the holy word,
Prepared to unravel unknown secrets:
Mildew on the curtain the same perchance
As a minstrel's chord deeming sovereignty
Where the film allusively o'er romance
Obscures the rose known as intimacy.

A lief no more who longs in wonderment
Vain lines that have no accompaniment.

68

The Mirror Held Up to Sanity

Look where the pale light of a heavenly body
is presented on a plane which can't be touched . . .

each momentary shift
the reverse of its counterpoint in the heart
which has retreated
from little to nil
and thus returns
to events preceding stepping onto the beach.

Am I a wanderer in a fruitless search
for paradise,
the effortless absence of suffering

ergo, with no vital confluence
with the power
which passes from clouds
to tree
to grass
and luminescent reflections?

Have I the wisdom
to wait
until hearing the breeze ushered by deity
greater than my idea of divinity . . .

and lean forward an inch . . .

to where there's no boundary to light thrown
from the orb and light on ardor
to brush into the structure
of canvas and pigments
the coursing of the moon through night-time skies

and the people who dwell within the intangible diffusion.

Self-Perpetuation

I may lift a ball,
place it in a cylinder,
rotating it until I am bored

what I will continues on until the task
is ended.

The moon
may drift to paradise
while the Gorgon stares into my eyes
turning me to stone

what I feel
is only of limited duration.

I can read a line
in ether
as if an angel delivered in ecstasy
or an amanuensis cast from eons ago,
his pen scratching the paper

what I witness could have arisen
as the mortified cough
of a demon transposed
in numinous empathy falling in shadows
and blood
until it arrives as the word of a saint

But the I witnessing "I",
because of the clarity perceived
in illuminating its revelation,
undiminished by doubt sustaining its being,
must persevere beyond the limited boundaries
of its own,
in accordance with the "I" heard,
felt and uttered within, creative act
in the moment
into eternal dimensions without perishing

as I am witness to the entirety of this act.

70

Heretical

I sat here waiting
till they believed in your name

you never came and I died listening to your echo.

There is no end to the One

even we cannot reduce infinitude.

Nothing can limit the totality

even our desire for independence.

Nothing can restrict the orchestration of magnitude

including our need
to think
we are self-contained.

There is nothing other

and we belong

within.

Spinozahuis
Rijnsburg
Netherlands

71

Immanence

The door opens
to a path which winds toward an arbor

rain spatters the leaves

I'll rest for some time,
wonder whether the trickles
upon the woodwork will reach the ground
before my heartbeat increases
at your approach

settle in your lap, my dearest

you, who above all else,
must really be

who breathes into my ear
must feel the same as I do

invigorated
by an overarching divinity
emptying love into each soul,
charging us with the verve
to find one another
lest we remain enchanted
in the storm building in the clouds
we know may drive a keen suitor
from our dreams.

72

New Jerusalem

In a vague, ill-defined future
separated from breathing, sweating humanity
who have no capacity to delve into its secrets?

With us, not obviously in the crossroads
of the city,
but askance somewhere
that isn't recognized as here and now?

With loving attention to detail,
integrating form
and function,
ensuring that color, shape and texture
are unified in one glorious appraisal
of heavenly splendor,
and reflected to the sighted
who'll believe they'll stand at the threshold
between mundanity
and supernal being?

Gold
for his halo,
porcelain for his untarnished visage

swirling cascades
for his locks,
a spiral staircase for the ascension to his abode

angels
to serve, a face to descry wonder

rays to bless
with light,
a child at the apex

a heart innocent
as the morn breaking on towers
that have no standing elsewhere
than in the vision
of a lonely apostle
who has the eyes to see.

Dekanatspfarrkirche
St Johann in Tirol
Austria

73

Long Gone

The shaman
willed us to deny each other

an arrowhead
found its mark, blood dripped
in the snow exfoliating like a chrysanthemum

warriors gathered on the plain.

Your body
haunts the darker realms

a droplet lands,
a silent draught rearranges your smile,
your breath touches my face

the distant wind circles.

I see you hiding
amongst the leaves

pray for repairing the distance
which remains between us.

Shanghai
China

74

God Speaks through Things

I am not blind
to great things

they pulsate with rhythm and love.

I am not conditioned
to receive grace from an extra-terrestrial source

the rise of the sun
is enough to inspire me
to following a course
set by its magisterial workings.

I am not indebted to a sacred text
for every act of kindness

the natural wellspring
is enough to impel me to support my brethren.

But whatever I think,
in moments of creative expression,
is nothing compared to a sunset
which resounds with the glory of One
who has imparted all his good works
into the texture and flow
of the world I inhabit.

75

Freedom

Red,
a dutiful son's blood
on the field.

Blue,
the notion peace will rest within his bones.

White,
purity of intention to entomb his soul
in land that will never desecrate conscious impulses
in the name of sovereignty and leadership.

Stars to guide his countrymen
on the same path he trod,
stripes to count the times
they'll fall pursuing the greatest of achievements:

to map a direction
without interference from a mentor
who'd place wisdom at the service
of self-interest, yet espouse awe and respect
for each human who follows the course
assigned from the workings of the cosmos:

the inimitable singularity rising through the strivings
and fidelities of one nation,
the affairs of fellow citizens
who have heard the personal voice:

"Follow your own destiny."

                                                            Boston
                                          Massachusetts

Ennoblement

What is seen
in the meadow rises rapidly toward the mountain

its brethren,
who sit bewildered by its turn
of speed,
wait until they too
are impelled to lift beyond their instinct
and deny the brute need
that forces them to seek sustenance
as their only outlet
and pleasure:

an imperative that knows no other
than a greater being
than can be conceived
in the pasture
where they normally inhabit and await their death.

77

The Answer Is in the Thing Itself

I have dreamt of integrating thought
and matter,
of realizing a building's function
making it capable of existing
isn't merely manifesting an edifice
to the desires and whims
of pompous gravity,
but an eternal truth residing in the heart

fulfilled
in the instance
of the plan unfolding the principle:

the idea isn't abstracted
from the created object
countenanced within,
but arises as the preeminent calculation
of nature configuring and reconstituting her articulation
with human faculties at the center:

a door leads to the Kingdom of Heaven,
a staircase spirals as in the vine,
a child's room signifies peace, light
and the will to grow unencumbered
by the contrived needs of adulthood.

Schloss Jagerhof
Dusseldorf
North Rhine- Westphalia

78

Outside the Known World

A band of pearls stretched from a glistening brow
to the outer planets,
a radiant chorister expressing her will
to bend the world's orbit
into a timeless connection with Orion's heat,
a puissant caress in alliance with fragrance
from every flower cultivated under the sun.

Is there an answer,
a reply to the entreating
why humanity stands in isolation

a return from Heaven
when we beat against its membrane
with the questions:

Why do we deserve to die,
must we forsake beauty,
joy—

the noblest virtue, passionate rhythm—

to enter the Unknown
with no assurance of the Greatest Ideal?

When twilight covers every lighted candle
and the abyss buries nonchalance
under a tottering framework,
will we aspire even higher
beyond the flaking skin
and deadened eyes

or, with the parlance of a jester
caught up in the meaninglessness of folly,
submit to the luster
that threads between aching joints,
countenance droplets that fall and splash
in open palms

remain with a look of indifference
and a mantle of impotence?

79

Speak to Me of Higher Things

Hasten
before they come,
quicken your beating feathers
or they'll harness you
to naught

be sure of stepping lightly on the earth,
Will o' the Wisp

a gentle touch—

and flee.

They bear no ill will
but their look can poison
with need to see

eating not wondering.

Quickly

disappear out of reach,
catch the wind
where time leaves no imprint
and body rhythms follow patterns ruffling ether.

You have no way
of partaking
in the suffering.

80

No Escape

The glass has a crack which reaches from stem to rim.

Shall I drink the wine
or pour it down the drain?

The flower has lost its vital freshness
and color.

Is it still worthwhile to place it in a vase,
admire its aroma and shapely lines?

The heart
which once beat
every time a maiden walked by
is silent.

If, for a moment,
the buds swelled, the juice brimmed
and flesh between pasty skin
and colored bone
received a bolt from the tremoring sky,
would I sit up and take notice again?

The drapes hang heavily over the window,
the air between musty
like the back
of the chest of drawers.

Is it still worth looking at a moth
to see its movements under light
caught by the glare
and transfixed
or should I simply bypass the thing,
accept it as dead and gone
like a rock on a beach
or an encrusted insect in the window?

The Muse no longer speaks
in the manner
of a God,
emptying her imperatives
that guided me where luminous birds fluttered
out of range of the hunter's arrow,
dust burnished to a naked eye
glowed like sunlight,
the poppy seed exploded in remembrance
of an ideal flower
and unfurled for every seeker to find the center
of its delight.

Shall I bury every epistle
I have written
in mud, lie under the quilt
and merely presume to state what that fly
is thinking
when, incontinently raw and full of eggs,
it attempts to break through the glass,
find another mound

buzz out of my vision.

81

Bittersweet

All through summer
we sat by the stream running by

on fine evenings
listened to the drone of bees,
to the calling of the wood hen

as the day grew longer and a gloaming mist settled,
we whispered how the folding of twilight
into darkness
drew a fine line
between careful, distinct hearing
and the desire to exclaim
in rapturous summation
our immense joy in nature's bounty

taking time

to pack our things

and leave.

82

A Rarefied Atmosphere

November morning,
fields covered with snow,
a contemplative's prints
deep enough to leave a trail

another breath,
a puff
of white air

ten more yards,
parishioners who love life
to the full

a furnace reflected
in the window

drops
of sweat,
the glassmaker bringing forth another goblet

rich, dark soup
between two children
waiting for mother to ladle a portion

an unctuous fellow,
not normally granted responsibility,
given the task of ringing out the hour

a still monk who hasn't heard the bell
allowing his lips to crack,
breaking through dreams
and transcending awkward reticence:

A universe devoid of love
is like a stream
under the moon with no sparkle
on the ripples, a road high to the hills,
robbers waylaying a walker coming down
into the trees to greet his younger sister

or,
wherein no one can breathe
between skull bone and knee,
confinement lonely as burnt eggs.

A choice
to accompany the master:

on the heights
where the breeze
has left no trace of its beginning,
luminous pursuance
of unearthly stillness

or far below

things which oppose
and conflict
in expectation of their domination.

83

A New Generation

Consider a heart created from the beginning
without having developed
from something more primitive and simple,
its complexity once and for all time

and now, that its end has been reached,
it won't grow into something more aware
and illuminated as to its origin

what I feel and hope for?

Would I really want a finely proportioned object
if I could unfold into something more wise
and powerful and loving,
not merely in a blaze of glory on a distant plane,
but here,
eventually,
in this vale of suffering,
moving forward toward the God disclosed in the Text:

"Is it not written
in your own law,
replied Jesus,
I have said ye are gods?"

Will I fail to realize what I may become
because what is presumed to be static,
unchanging and once only

cannot surpass the fear
of being connected with all creatures on the earth

or,
as a highly efficient machine,
being greater,
as I was in the beginning,
than can be observed through the eyes
of flesh and gristle?

84

Mythical Journey

Footprints, pine needles crushed
on frozen trails,
blossoms scattered
beyond a vagabond's open arms,
the autumnal squall's insistence

a voluminous surge reaching the granite wall
as five,
no,
two gannets spiral

dry hands opening a letter
from the calligrapher:

have you
reached the light
shining
on
the waves,
the ice bound pinnacle,
rose tinted cumuli

satisfaction having come this far

a sword severing

(a bright glint)

the darkness
without harming
basic foundations?

Nikko
Japan

85

Inglorious Descent

In his citadel
the supreme artist submits before the blue wave
that carries him
where he can foresee each bone glazed
with fearlessness,
pure essence secreted though every gland
to sustain them
in perpetuity, the will that transcends impotence

ancient forces ascribing authorship
to the witness above sentiment
and need
to bow before another who claims holy might,
the mercurial paragon exceeding ordinary talent
as he conveys new lines
for intoxicated demons shouting for release:

No one can plummet as far
or taste the Sulphur as you

clamor against the window
of a spine

until I see fit,
only advancing into the light
when the time is ripe

the fruition
and Omega,
the end of all striving,
the last accomplishment rising
on gilded wings beyond the hierarchies intent
on punishment

the field on which he lies, clutching his ankle

so close to the edge

moreover,
the fall taking his life

the pulped mess at the foot of the hill.

86

An Equivalence

Even when
there seems no harmony between this dimension
and another far surpassing the perimeter
inborn
in an outward thrust to become beyond itself
it can be heard clearly they belong together
through the very fact that what gives one breath, love
and desire subsists in the other to the same degree,
what binds one also binds its opposite:

the dance on waves signifying disease
and a lion-hearted beat,
the fistula
and the smooth transition from a baby's nape
to Satchitananda,
the leap from agape
to erotic meandering through dense forests
and the morning sun within

what constitutes you
also constitutes me,
what feels pain in the zone
I can see
also shudders in a breast light years away

whoever passes the extreme limit
and returns anew,
distanced from myopia with a quizzical grin,
will leave a trace of this world
in the otherness
that can' t be fathomed by ordinary eyesight.

87

Something to Think About

I have no certainty
when the maid who promised a churn of cream returns
I will caress her face the following hour
as I said I would this morning,
no guarantee
when the dove coos from one window,
lights on rafters and flies off into the blue sky,
I will see it again

(I could at any moment expire
like a flame when it reaches the end of the match)

cannot be certain when the priest passes the door
he will think of me as he would someone he loved

(for all I know he may revile me
because I don't fit his standard of holiness)

cannot be sure the moaning in the asylum
I visit on Wednesdays
will not enter a higher pitch
as I step
in the corridor
that has no air holes
or light bulb.

What use are my achievements
and goals, ambitions
and pride, loves
and joys

the countryside
in bloom, the pealing of the fine bell
in the monastery,
the trellis covered with honeysuckle?

For a moment I shall draw down the blind,
place a cold match on the sideboard

renew the urgency
of discovering who sits in the corner smoking his pipe ,
imploring the past to stop before it begins

contemplating extinction.

88

IDENTITY

I try to find the reason
why I live

the question
Who am I?
that at any moment I'll cease to be
before knowing who I am.

Who
is this I?

No thing?

Who am I?

A heavenly agent
who blossoms in spring like a wet lotus
and transfigures dust into a kind
of paste no one can eat or see?

A man of letters
whose intention to inscribe his name
on effort enshrines the same name in the tomb,
who follows the pulse of his own blood
and the flow
of his own lymph,
one
of many.

A vital organ that counts backwards
from infinity
and forward from zero,
who defines space between yesterday
and tomorrow
as now
and between eyebrows black common sense?

A vagabond,
notwithstanding the dictation of sweat
and toil
to surface
and drown his song, inevitably,
who translates an ancient script signifying the mighty deeds
of heroes into his own faltering step,
into his own uncoordinated wanderings,
in order to discover who blinds the eye
with grey blood and beguiles the heart
into pretending it has no answer?

89

Conscience

If I pull a wing from a fly and watch it buzz around,
constrained by its inability
to lift off the ground

(how it buzzes,
intolerably disillusioned by the void
on its right side)

would I surrender to the same inability
to divine a path past the intolerable stench
if my arm were missing,
dream of faraway places where abandonment
is my lot, do anything I please
with no fear of consequence,
untrammeled by duty
float free of responsibility,
spiraling into archaic emporiums against the apex

(eyelids stuck together)

or,
perchance,
choose to do what I hear,
resoundingly
and without contention within:

"Stick that fly's wing on again."

90

God with Us

What if
there isn't a throne
with choirs announcing your approach
and you wander a darkened corridor

when eyes no longer glimpse the moon's rise
on a frosty night,
and close irreparably,
the panorama transforms
into a discoloration
of your face lying prone looking upward

water
trickling to your skull turns into little drops
and patters on interminably?

Would you worship the transcendent being
who floats on ether
impervious to calls for supplication,
would you cry out in triumphant joy
that his reign has penetrated to your feet,
would you address Him
as conqueror, righteous hero,
the God
for everyone

or,
would you,
like me,
care to see him standing in the rubble
and stooping to lift a child that had lost its limbs?

91

A New Dawn

What I am unable to express
you can utter it for me,
when I can no longer sense the immediate impact
of my world
you can guide me
to the place which heals

when the vast organon,
which has allocated a place to a shadow
of my former self, alleviates pressure
on the strand between assent and forward momentum
you can place my hand
where it can turn formlessness
into a useful object.

Notice the light
from our candles reflecting in the other's eye,
and that same glow conjuring a myriad
of potentialities reflects in one's own

the revelation of the hierarchies furthering my destiny,
with the same luminous impulse, articulates yours

the voice
I remember which guided me
to you
is the same calling you received leading you to me.

Slowly,
then,
as the darkness enters an even sharper contrast
against concerted emanation
and sympathy
of intention is found between us,
we'll proceed to the brow of the hill
where our presence will be discerned more clearly

each figure delineated
with an ever-increasing clarity.

The inception of Camphill
Newton Dee
Aberdeen
Scotland

92

Awake

Immobile,
a statue before the world
steady
each breath poised on the next
as if no one other may interfere
with the stillness
motionlessness,
steady
the moon above a canyon,
a shadow
the light obscured from reaching rock,
placidity
the sky at peace

all is still . . .

Dedicated to Ansel Adams

93

Mutual Assent

I have no recollection
we met on a trail
through the mountains
and you gazed at me

my vision touched by your lovingness.

I can't remember having met
near a temple
by a river with the sun beating down,
you speaking and asking who I was
or whether I knew from where thoughts came
or from whom they were addressed
when they seemed ridiculous
and of no importance.

I do recall, however, I found you in a dream
after you died,
and the tone like a long-forgotten echo
still meant something to me:

I am
where the heart is.

I belong where you cannot see

but listen:

You are where the heart is. I am
where the heart is too.

                                          Dedicated to Ramana Maharshi

94

A Jazz Band Somewhere in the Corner

Find the bar
and exalt greater knowledge

love

eyes where tones and melody merge
in twilight counting each star.

"Another, please."

Everything I do is preceded
by my ancestors

I live in their shoes
and repeat their mistakes

if only I could transcend their differences
and recreate destiny anew

unveil the ghost
behind my liver contemplating inanity
and yesteryear's indifference, humming
on an empty street,
a whistle in my pocket and no shoes . . .
"How about a dime, mister."

We'll live to see the resurrection,
the final curtain raised,
the immanent act
circularly in repentance

embodied sainthood emulating patterns
of a cosmos in formation.

"Last drink, guys"

Who was the Son?
Have I the capacity to remember?
Was he blessed?
Am I blessed

can I sense his talent in another era, another body

transmute his pain,
the loss of his mother, the faithlessness?

Lift my spirit. Shine,
oh Son.
You'll take me back.
Return me to the heart,
to the long-lost loving stroke of genius.
Polish my shoes.
Keep up my socks.

95

American Dream

Will power isn't determined solely by the need
to speak out for the sake of injustice
nor by reason uncovering a cause motivating it
to address an issue and fight it

our hearts
are no place for inertia.

We can have no party with grandiose ambitions
and schemes

they are not enough to overcome the malady
of the night conspiring with inequality.

Ours must be with the highest, most loving,
noble spirit that transcends indignity.

Ours must be with the hallowed,
all surpassing intention
which has only peace and the right
of humanity to live in harmony
as its guiding light
and ideal.

Ours
is not to say,
"*I* have done it
or achieved it
out of desire to imprint my name
on history, sacrificing intimate fellowship
for a better world

but the spark of the divine,
which has risen on behalf of mankind,
is alive
in my breast

enough to make me feel
no other can extinguish it
for the sake
of their own inability
to find it in themselves.

96

Maharishi

What you possess is finite, untranslatable
into transcendence
and holiness that far surpasses worldly gain.

What you hanker for as you envisage a place of security
and comfort is a figment of desire to be the one
with things that avoid your true calling:

a brother to the helpless,
a friend to the worthless and a Samaritan
to the beggar who asks you for a copper to assuage his hunger.

What, however,
is higher calling
is the blessed given from the very ground
that supports and guides you

the need
to show you belong
to One who has already assumed the mantle
of guru and Lord,
who will make things easier than your own fumbling
for enlightenment and transcendental calm.

What you will gain will be parodied
by outsiders whose surreal countenances,
dishonestly serving their own accomplishment,

pass by the grace that could be theirs
if they surrendered for one moment unto One
whose breath and fiber
is suffused with the invigorated youthful belief
he can influence others for the good.

97

Mother

When there is no air, I shall breathe liquid love

no earth to stand on,
climb the stair
made out of finely tuned notes
resounding from your throats

and, when there are no words
to tell of how the flame glows
and aspires

merely smile.

98

NEW AGE

Whatever we have done
to disturb patterns that preceded entrance into the temple

we renounce it.

Whenever we feel lonely and disturbed
by heartache sundering youth from the spring

we shall take up instruments and pronounce with vigor
the flow that always surrounds the individual:

one for Buddha and his wisdom,
two for Allah
who we know in the depth of sincerity
will deliver us
from languor stultifying in inertia
the act of ultimate renewal,
three for Jesus
who broaches hatred with tenderness and mercy

four for Krishna
who will lead us to avow:

We are happy in your presence,
joyful in your abode.
Hare Hare Hare.
Hare Rama Hare Hare.

We dance, we sing.
We are the blessed ones.
We adore beauty.
We pray

we weep while we follow

while we serve

devoted to thee

Krishna

Hare Hare Hare
Krishna hare.

99

Intruder

I no longer participate extensively in your affairs
or accost with summations of prowess,
yet I could enliven your quick
and provide an even more hallowed countenance
to observe the ground filtering between your fingers
contains more than what you see
when you turn it toward light:

echoes
of centuries reminding where you stand
evokes a similar pattern,
although
where acorns litter the path
you herded swine,
while now taste their bitter juice,
the same scent that gorged the nostrils
of one seeking their fill,
allowing the pulpy center to divulge a question:

What will I be
when every loose strand
is gathered into one exclamation
that precedes clinging to the surface?

The candid,
dark, simply untouched by wanton fingers,
completely absorbent space,
the unrestricted, yet fully aware intention
to escape the confines and proceed toward the sun . . .

higher than a mountaineer's print
not yet melted,
but only visible if one drains sugary fluid
from the pipe connecting Antares
and Lucifer's backbone

the immobile stretch tessellated by extra human joiners,
who have no inkling of the savagery
of one who dwells under the polar star light years away,
that reveals
I have nowhere else to go
when the shadow catches up and engulfs me . . .

despite the empty chalice no one could grasp,
excess of absence, the dormant,
nearly involuble speech no one wanted to hear

the barely lit opening that makes one feel
nothing will stop a new for from appearing…

mordant dewdrop spliced on ice,
filaments
of green rivulet green
embalmed in swathes falling from clouds

the pursed lipped denouement:

"I have no home anymore,
my abode is where angels swoop and remonstrate:"

"He really doesn't belong here."

100

Peace Be with You

A caress on a cheek by a loved one,
a warrior battling two headed dragons
which ripped at the sinews
between ankle
and knee bone,
a butterfly landing on a forehead
turned upward to a disappearing moon,
an adamant expression
in the breast of a soothsayer:

"Don't regret the passing,
a yellow bloom will enter your dreams again."

A mild breeze reaching eyelids
in the afternoon's drowsy heat,
an iron rod standing silently by the path
that leads from the mine's network of tunnels
to an old well,
a night charm
in ardor on a maiden's arm
which loves to sweep unobtrusively
in silken haberdashery

a brightly lit interior
wherein each word
in the dialect
of sainthood
is spoken afresh.

'With One Eye Open,' is an account of the wanderings of Jobe Havelock in England, Scotland, and Wales. Jobe has submitted notes and poems to me, which I have arranged in an order, I hope, adequately reflects the correct sequence of events and thoughts. Jobe would like to thank the people he met on his journey who inspired him to continue, even though an outcome is never certain and, he assures me, an outcome may never really be the heart's desire. Amongst many, in particular, he mentioned the guide at Gloucester Cathedral who, with enthusiasm and love, pointed out the cloisters where monks had written daily in half-light through stained glass; the old man he sat with at Glencoe, discussing the wildlife thereabouts; the schoolteacher he met, only for a short time, in Pembrokeshire, who studied Joseph Conrad and decided the author wrote from where patience is born. A journey never ending, only deepening in its exclusion of that which corrupts an ability to be receptive to all that is good in the universe.

101

With One Eye Open

The trail between Bushey and the M1 passes fields which spread between housing estates and an international university where, one would presume, answers are attempted to solve problems as old as humanity itself. Why did that child have to suffer needlessly? Why did the Creator leave us to fend for ourselves if, with a simple reconstitution to the good, we could have escaped degradation and despair?

> There are flowers which appear to become lost
> in color and identical blooms,
> each reflecting the other's need
> to survive and face the hazy sky.
> There is a tree standing alone,
> waiting for spring
> to fully reveal its loveliness and ability

> to withstand the ages
> of neglect
> and disinterest.
> There are thorns and brambles which only tear the skin
> and make you feel alienated
> from the world
> and vulnerable on the path.
> There is someone listening to the birds,
> watching the sky,
> and wondering why he feels so separate.

Winter shadows dapple the roadway as Jobe approaches Glencoe. The misery inflicted upon women and children who dared to uphold honorable tradition still conveys a mournful reminder of cruelty. He stands beside a river and peers at the hills surrounding the valley— so bleak, so bereft of foliage, the earth protrudes through the turf and forbids luxuriance. The ripple over the stones sounds as cold as a drumbeat in snow, or a cockatrice abandoned by a lover. He cannot understand why they did it. Beneath the pebbles there is a bone washed clean now by centuries of fresh water straight from the heights. It could have been a little girl's, or an old man's. It came off before it needed to, and lodged there against its will. So easy to speculate on death and pretend he could have experienced it in a dream, and the resonance will pervade his nightmares and unholy visions. But the truth is, he cannot, even in his most sincere and penetrating glimpses into past action, ever hope to fathom how generosity could turn into bloodshed, and the malevolent gaze on an innocent child bring forth the imperative to annihilate its breath and render it senseless.

He follows the road toward Loch Carron past burns and ridges that jut into the foreshore.

> You could watch all evening
> and not see a fish break the surface,
> which will remain calm and unaffected
> by the claims we make on nature

to provide us with clues
as to the reason why we suffer.

Look deeper into your own disquiet
and wonder whether its source is a malevolent force
or an unconscious course
where one state surpasses another
and, in turn,
is taken over by another

a valley raised by an earthquake,
a red coat beaten to death as he rode a fine horse on his way to church,
a dove's spiral flattened
by a gust from the hill

an ongoing falling
and rising,
absorbing and displacing each other's opposite.

Overnight a storm from the west uprooted a tree. Waves pound the shoreline, visibility is obscured. Nowhere outside is free to withstand the gale. A clock on the mantlepiece ticks; he has no use for punctuality. A fan from an ancient culture obscures a corner; he desires no air to revitalize his skin. The scent of soap fills the room; he contemplates the passerby who would wash his feet. A wastepaper bin sits under the desk; he declines to crumple and throw in his notes.

Jobe takes a train back to London where the hustle and shove can be a joy or torment. Yet, it is not as busy as usual. The tourists have disappeared, and even Londoners aren't about. He strolls Thames Embankment without much interest in the Houses of Parliament which line the river. His immediate concern— Shalmaneser's eldest son, who designed the ziggurat reaching the moon separating one point of view from another, columns of steel zigzagging across an ashen backdrop, bibulous ghosts draining fluid from an ageing network of canals, an inconsequential second making for a seat to settle.

The wind
has dropped to nil and the pavement is oily black:

I have no demand
to create a worldly edifice
and transform poverty
into earnest success or valiant failure.

The damp penetrates each layer
of clothing:

I will assume a destiny that transcends worldly issues
and deliberation on policy that keeps the wheel turning
toward wealth
and fortune.

Light reaches its object instantly
and reflects it back:

Night is my repose and the elixir for my endeavor.
It is where I'll address my concern
and extricate the long loving line
that I am under no coercion to join,
but can remain on the outside looking in
and on the path glancing askance.

The buds have rejuvenated after winter's dormancy, and he finds himself again in the lanes of Hertfordshire. Jobe often takes a path which leads to Letchmore Heath where Bhakti Vedanta Manor, the temple for the Hare Krishna Society, is situated. In their gardens you come across little plaques inscribed with quotes from the Bhagavad Gita. The people are contemplative, thoughtful and polite. They provide free vegetarian meals and express the greatness of the Godhead with analogies and benign gestures. Ducks fly onto the pond, leaving wakes that slowly ripple to the edges. It is as if the wisdom and spirit of India has arisen in the woods of middle England. Jobe is not averse to reading their scriptures, if it means the Holy Transcendence can penetrate to his quick and transform him.

>
> At the end of the trail there could be a blessing
> or a curse depending on the manner
> in which we pass through shadows
> and dappled furrows.
> At the extreme limit of the path
> there could be blindness to illusion
> or edification that what one has done
> has been in accordance with wisdom
> and virtue
> and not one's limited view on things.
> Now, however, as the journey is in mid step,
> the venal moon proffered
> unto the reign of an ubiquitous sun preceding the advent
> of your own folly,
> one embodies yesterday in the marrow of now,
> as if it did indeed belong inside jelly and water
> or, in air sweet as sylvan lip scent outside the bone,
> casts glances at an eternal livery
> far from the mundane parlance of a sedentary voyeur.

Summer has arrived on the Pembrokeshire coast. The days are longer, the grass warmer, and the sky seems to recede into distances only a god could caress when he is bored. Jobe sits on a hill watching a cloud. He would, if he could, join its voluminous expanse and rain upon all creatures below. But it is so white, any thoughts of precipitation dry into negligence. He plucks a stalk and places it between his lips. It tastes of the desert in Samarkand and is as hard as a spike lifted to defend against unwanted incursions.

As far as one could deliver pinpricks in a royal mantle,
to the constellation outside human vision traducing blindness
with snippets of feral light,
a flower sends its odor:

the glutinous echo bearing down upon a neophyte
awaiting communion
with an ecstatic pallbearer's plenipotential spirit
conveyed from a blazing garden:

"I am just out of reach."

Through subsoil underlying an alchemist's need
to glean elements
for experiments embodying dead flesh with glittering numen,
not only through loneliness encountering the same eyes
returning its own forsaken stare,
but the mortal tear between sanity and idleness,
a moist filament enters the collusion
of smoldering ash
and an oozing coelothant's bodily fluid:

the pearlescent gulf separating the martyr
from execution
is equal
unto the time you think it takes to build an edifice
to a great artist's achievement.

The waning sun and rising moon, falling air and rising dew. Jobe is uncertain where to look. Beneath copper-brown leaves, in an ant's nest, where the gulls surrender their desire to scream for another tidbit, in the eye that searches diligently for a clue to the whereabouts of the red suffusing the horizon?

If I can be everything, I must be it

and you taste the edges,
and she dips her finger in lava,
heat that never diminishes

and I scream till it shakes your temple,
my choice leaving no choice but to suffer eternally.

I am everywhere,
drinking color from every glance upturned toward light
and, where nothing can grow,
draining the spent hue into apathy

and you try to accompany me.

Autumn passes into another Hertfordshire winter— so cold this year, the temperature has dropped to -14 degrees. Jobe accompanies people who require special assistance on their walk across the fields to purchase trinkets and sweets from the local farm shop. At night he joins them for supper, and lights candles in mock grottoes, celebrating the return of light from one season to another. He has befriended a young woman whose temper and disposition to argument frustrate his longing for a conflict free relationship. In a college library he discovers a book by Rudolf Steiner, entitled, "Karmic Relationships:". Within, he reads that any antagonism has at its source an event in a previous life— his life, his disobedience, his empty vows, his malignancy.

As deep as a snowdrop in a hedge,
as pure
as cloud light when first it falls,
as soft as a newborn's eyelid,
as white as . . .

willingness to find you in it,
to dig
until I discover your hands already numbed
before it came down,
to lift your head
and caress it,
to touch your lips . . .

to find you where I left you
with three broken fingers and a pulse rapidly failing.

Now the ice will harden, but
I will still hear your voice:

"It is still, so silent.
Accompany me
to the One
who entrusted you to find me again."

A day off and a walk where he will, Jobe enjoys seeking out back streets away from tourist traps and extraordinary events planned to draw the crowds. Along the Grand Union Canal he has seen a 19th Century barge, the remains of a crane still protruding over oily water and a discarded newspaper, whose headlines react about a soccer victory the country has witnessed the other night. Before him rise the structures of the gasworks and the back of St Pancras Station. One of his treats is to listen to the trains as they pass, and eventually to catch one, speeding toward a station covered with creepers that had grown there since he first visited London three years ago.

> I adore the buds and the shrubs
> and trees bursting into new life.
> I can smell the freshness even though the fumes
> of a great city taint the shadows.
> I can watch unmolested,
> jump for joy,
> if I like, and pretend,
> for a moment,
> that any deeds wrought in the confines
> of determination to succeed,
> which have brought suffering,
> and any sense of worthlessness
> and anxiety are obliterated,
> because I am alive and well.

Blackpool in the summer: walks along the promenade, fish and chips, rides in old trams; the accent of the north— heavy, full of "luv" and "duckie"; the steady beat of the fair ground in the distance, and water up to your ankles. Blackpool in the summer, where guesthouse landlords invite you to accompany another holiday maker from the breakfast table.

Jobe sets out alone to wander the sand, wondering how far the tide had receded, and whether anything lives in the rivulets that are left— quite deep they seem. The air is gentle and mild. Seabirds gather nearby, and squawk at each other, intent on securing a meal if thrown their way. The tang in his nostrils reminds him of bladder wrack on deserted isles, and of Phoenician vessels that proceed daily into the Hellespont, past idols of marble and triremes packed with slaves. If there were a temple where he could praise the Heavens for such a beautiful day, then the blue dome above would be fittingly apt for its roof, and the pillars of clouds to the east appropriate columns holding it in place.

Each globule of water,
each fish that swims from the ledge beneath the waves,
and each child
that awaits an afternoon shaft of sunlight
is said to have been made
with the Word.
Every rock
and grain
I have witnessed near the edge,
and touched with gentleness and care,
has been bought into being
with the sound ringing in my ears:

"You are
and I am."

The October wind is chill as Autumn itself. It circulates the grounds of Gloucester Cathedral where Jobe would present his thoughts to Jesus Christ, not for the first time. A sprinkle of rain reflects back the pale light of the morning. Cars slide past on their way to places he will never visit or ponder about, so quickly their reason must be an imperative which far surpasses his own immanent incursions. The door of the Cathedral is open, and on a whim he enters the darkened enclosure. A well-dressed family gathers around a small coffin, and an old priest is holding a service. Jobe sits in the back row. A sob in the corner, a trickle in the drainpipe, a cough . . .

"Unburden her soul in the Eternal Father
who awaits her in Paradise.
Whatever trial she underwent,
whatever pain usurped her desire
to lead a fulfilling and worthy life,
all will be brought into the mellow breath
and revealing aura of the transfigured one
in holier that holier otherness.
Her greatest doubts
will be overturned in purity,
her deepest fears
will be transformed into an elevated sense of well being,
and her ignorance of the meaning
of association with betterment and valor
will be translated into the union that has no bounds,
and, when the veil falls and darkness clouds her every fiber,
a real presence will start to exclaim,
"You are in my love.""

"To where will you go next? When will the journey end?" are questions I am always asking of Jobe. Bemused, he usually replies: "Where the spirit takes me," and, "It won't".

This revision of Jobe's wanderings concerns his refusal to stay put in one place; no one can share his lonely desire to find the reason why he belongs more in the forgotten past than in the present, things still haunt him from afar—storm engraved outcrops, a sandbar, a melaleuca tree in the rain. They evoke responses, as if he were their author, replying to his own call through the centuries. "What did I do then? Was I the cause of that malignancy, of that joy?"

In discovering Tasmania, Jobe found here, too, voices from the past were his to capture and respond to, voices so obscure they appeared only to be blown in the wind, or brought up in the froth and bubble of the tide. Jobe, however, is convinced they are directed to him and, ultimately, will provide clues to his identity, albeit a sensitive and poetic one.

102

A Window without Glass

Who would he like to meet on a coast where no one seems to visit when the wind is so strong it threatens to blow him into another dimension unpeopled by robbers or saints? Who would value accompanying him to the furthest point where the surf my strike a vagabond and drench him from head to foot? Jobe has found himself alone, again, on a Sunday afternoon, with no one to talk to on the beauty of the environment he can perceive into the distance.

Would this piece of earth, South Arm and the beaches forming its outline, have witnessed the new surpassing the ancient, allowing a notion to seep into its odors and plant life? Would the source of the well sought in bedrock and salt have been retained as a record in the rising and falling dunes, layers of sand upon shells, and in pits dug by hands covering their tracks?

There is whispering in the air and a message concentrated
in the waves:

You were not the first
to gaze upon this shore
nor will you be the only one wondering why its hues are deep,
rich, and profoundly moving.

There's melancholy
in the sand and a voice of sadness in the wind:

"I'll never see it again
nor taste the salt or feel the water wash against my thighs."

There's a personal note in the spray
and a monotonous tone ringing around my ears:

"Centuries built the contours, seconds may destroy them
and love could build them up again."

Unanswered cries for restitution,
tenderness borne on ether, blue, surf and sun.

All too much for an ordinary man on the headland.

Jobe walked to D'Entrecasteaux Channel where he heard that Aboriginal tribes had inhabited the area, meeting an end on a small settlement at Oyster Cove. Eight or nine people sitting very still and looking fixedly at the camera.

      Spilt piping sky tones, yellow wattles,
          swooping from the east

          eggshells scattered
           on the rocks
and pulpy white flesh washed by waves ashore,
            in abeyance
before they curl over and rush against open limbs

          salt in the sea,
salt in a womb, gore-streaked wake subsiding

          bones aligned
with shadows cast from where stained fur overlaps vulnerable flesh,
          dew soaking moss,
    vascular effulgence brooding actual light

         errant scratches
          in undergrowth,
           grey bands,
    night mulch dampening pads,
    scent keeping to obscurity

red raw scratches at the moon spilling frozen white drops
           on higher ground,
     milk left for the young to swallow
the same as welling from a daughter's globes

stealth in the hunt, the meaty taste of prey.

He passes houses built to command views over the river; wide expanses of glass reflecting light that shines and sparkles on the waves. He makes his way to the water's edge and sits beneath a she-oak overlooking the swell and retreat of the sea. A hand brushes away a fly, a foot pushes at a pebble, the moon is faint like a wisp of smile on a blue afternoon sky; the devil is incarnate, so conspicuous he could be hunted through susurrating veins in orbit around a bloated head and pastel motion slowed down.

The tide has brought three things
to remember:

a rifle butt clubbing a man on the head,
eyes watching naked figures dancing by the sea,
and prayers of thanksgiving
for having escaped the brute force of waves into the cove.

The tide will take back three things to consider
when the young and conscionable return
to look into the tangle and bewilderment of folly,
asking over and again.

Can the sea wash clean sorrow
as it does the hands after murder?
Does it feel our secret desires
and hold them in perpetuity?
Is its surge against our will to survive only to become greater
as we enter further with our heads claiming we know its secrets?

Jobe follows the road further south, just about far as possible to go south, near to the end of the world. He assumes that in reaching an absence of friction and irresponsibility, he may encounter the evidence that he belonged here, he could erect a dwelling and call it home, as so many others have done. But there is a sense of dissatisfaction, a foreboding: to put down roots would be where he didn't belong. Unless peace were made with the spirit singing over the waves, he would need to counter it with disbelief, erudition, or self-interest that binds to forces of magnitude and idolatry; that weeps not for blood spilt in vain, nor for the echo swirling around his knees at sunset.

Turmoil will return
when waves from the sea bring debris and froth,
division
will occur when a forceful wind cracks branches
and lifts trees

when every blemish
in an otherwise tranquil evening
are discerned as notes
in the swell and diminution of a lingering song,
unease will take the place of self-possession:

"I could stay only for a while,
my journey superseded by others
who'll suffer even more from the change
that turns brain stuff,
liver,
spittle and hair into flecks undulating on the wind,
and the limpid eye which can see a brother's lineaments
in the decay and outgrowth
of pith and fiber,
into an organ that calculates the gain to be made
from replacing a shared outlook
with an exclusive viewpoint."

Calm, as if a divine overseer had gently brushed the landscape with the ability to diminish cruelty, superstition and the impairment of human resilience envisioning the cause of suffering.

He would like to convey his gratitude in this moment of tranquility, for the gnawing disappointment that he doesn't belong anywhere of importance has receded, as has the cry of a seagull into the horizon. Whatever he has done to share in dispossession and degradation is being alleviated; for, without the urgency of need to contain this vista in perpetuity, the freedom to turn in any direction, and find this moment again, will be his.

Even though obedient to the demands
of an unending cycle on a surface
which intimates nowhere can be devoid
of an edge between itself and what it isn't,
as the worldly recedes
and the eternal encroaches,
hues mellow and devolve
from another where

feelings are as deep as distance to the horizon,
water is stained with vital fluid,
air is breath, and the absence
of disquiet is why you hear a resonance in the sand
and tears
in the wash calling for an undefiled land.

Yellow— the day's length absorbed into the sun's disappearance. Pink— the vital well giving up its secret that it obeys a higher order of existence. Orange— memory that lingers when all vision terminates in anticipation of the blackest night.

Despite an agreement with the soil not to defile it, with the water not to stagnate it, and with the hills and valleys not to denude them, he still doubts his capacity to tend to the earth as if could have been, lovingly, so it retained the freshness and nourishing capacity it had a thousand years ago. The responsibility would be too deep and awesome.

> I am only passing by
> and the little I do to exploit its riches,
> dependent solely on its grace
> and goodwill to render unto me
> what sustains me and keeps me alive,
> would not give back what made it fruitful.

Morning.

> There is no movement

> even the seagull poised in solitude echoes a stationary observer
> who denies the potential
> for disruption.

> As limpid as a freshwater fish's eye
> through the surface to the light above

> grains
> of white sand identifiable separately.

> As near to balance
> estimable by an uneven heartache

mathematical configurations no doubt have pertinence,
but not here at this time.

As silent as nature in retreat,
the blooming mollusk
at dawn,
or the tadpole in flight

a reverie easily broken by the demand of an ordinary man
to place himself on the landscape and call it his own.

He is confronted with the unalterable reality that no matter how much he treasures a piece of land, no matter how much he adores its beauty, odors and plant life, he must inevitably lose it when he dies. Its grittiness, harsh contours, and texture like the back of his hand, will, in the manner of dandelion fluff on a breeze, be blown to extremities that a man burdened with the heaviness of mortal need could never chase or catch up to.

A non-entity such as a dream has no edges or structure,
and no rhythm
or abundance of foam, salt
and grit between cracks.

An ethereal presence, like the aftermath
of tenderness expressed in an act of kindness,
doesn't seem so noticeable
when the sound
of waves pounding rocks
and the roar of wind reaches the upper air.

The movement of blood, lymph
and moisture through fatty tissue
is never as noticeable as the descent of a branch through foliage
and onto the plants beneath,
nor is the fear of being seen without credibility,
an identity
or a loved one
as acute as the reaction
that fathoms one headlong plunge
into nothingness.

A strong wind turns into rain and obscures his vision. Like the trail of a witch blinded by coal fire or a demented priest on the loose after having stolen artifacts from the altar, he is caught in a storm which threatens to force him off his ground. What would it take to wash him into the sea, to cut him with kelp, and to send him to the bottom in love with the view, peering at his own inert frame for eons?

After the rain
another burst will occur.
Thunderclap after thunderclap.
Across the world, so it seems.
An emissary from the Gods
who know no love or compassion?
The surging past of memory?
A face in the wind—
split lips and bruised skin.
Another unholy deed?
Unthinking,
insentient force?
The rage of an overseer who denies denial?
It cleanses the surface and disowns the fixated.

It ended abruptly as it began. Jobe climbs into the hills overlooking Bruny Island, and gazes at the purple aftermath disappearing beyond Cape Raoul.

It is possible to hear birds calling one another
from distances greater than usual,
to identify their plumage in light bursting through clouds
only to disappear
and reveal an instant later
a brilliance surpassing its former manifestation

now yellow, blue
then white again,
or hardly discernable flickering into absence

likewise, the uncertainty of life itself,
whose deeds may have been brought forth in folly,
misdemeanor
and crazy action fostered in denial of civility,
will return again only in a different form,
either with an insidiously more decadent aspect
or lit up
by forgiveness
and mitigated by honesty.

Jobe returns to the shoreline.

He sits in the lea of a boulder, and waits. How close is he to the wave beneath, the sucking and the rush? Will it dislodge him from here? What would he relinquish to save himself from its relentless drive? He would that he wouldn't stare at his own image and treasure slipping along fancily in need of forever. He would that he wouldn't want to contain it because he cannot bear its upheaval. He would that he could be protected by hearing its will before it occurs, because he listens as if it were alive and not an insentient thing.

To focus on raindrops in summer heat
is to discover the ephemerality of things,
to delay repetition of a song into the wind
and hear it echo
is to prolong a sense of loneliness
before nature born of the question,
"From where?"
To stand in the building up of a winter storm,
and realize I am not capable of creating something so forceful
and wondrous
is to rediscover active individuality in the face of an elemental power
able to frustrate the ambitions
and motivation of the many who have decided that,
as tantamount only to an increase in desire for worldly given,
the evoking of an otherworldly force is neither beneficial
or necessary
to convey
how extraordinarily unearthly vitality fills an empty frame.

The air is fresh as any breathed by a swan on an ice floe, the colors stark as any drawn by a Zen master on white parchment, the light transparent as the finest day upon Saturn, and the sea silent as the lilt of a sleeper in bed with a loved one.

At least my ash
will replenish one flower.

"The voice of one crying in the wilderness," yet, one of concrete, girders and glass, is how I picture Jobe. New York City— brash, strident, almost overwhelming. New York State in deep autumn. He would like to stay for as long as he can afford, till the lure of another destination brings him out of the color and richness, which persists only a few miles out of the urban heartbeat.

103

A Vein to Paradise

Jobe visited an apartment which had been occupied by Thomas Wolfe, the author. A plaque on the outside indicated he had lived there while writing, "Of Time and the River", in the 1930s. If he had had the opportunity he may have like to have added, as an epitaph, the lines Jobe composed where he could look back on the skyscrapers of Manhattan:

> Here in the night
> without which there can be no sun,
> your weakness wasn't fame
> but a navel groping around for love
> like a puppet
> without strings.

Thomas Wolfe had called himself, "God's lonely man", and Jobe felt like this, walking the streets with little to accomplish. Yet there are moments when something worthwhile catches his attention: the buses letting down platforms to enable wheelchair bound people to alight, a shop window wherein an ivory statuette contrasted with motion behind him on the street— a Buddhist monk supporting his brother on his shoulders, with no staff or satchel, only a robe to partially cover their withered flanks.

In Central Park he remembered a piece of music arranged by Gary Mc Farland, entitled, "Reflections in the Park." The guest pianist was Bill Evans who, apparently, was constantly in need of heroin. Such fragile beauty out of such incarcerated need. It is as if God chooses his least obviously self-satisfied accompanists to invoke his most intimate structures in difference to perfection. The lines ripple against a background of shifting strings and delicate harmony.

> In discovering solitude
> where millions breathe and find time
> to challenge each other's space,
> the sound reveals incipient suffering
> only just staining margins
> and beating gently on the background
> to a singular, undistorted instant
> found in want of activity
> before the moon passes on
> from an ideal conjunction
> to a phase of disharmony
> and dispiritedness.

He takes a bus northward where maple and birch trees will be changing. Already he has seen a few orange and red leaves in New York, and wanted to experience the fall, sprinkling to the earth with the slightest breeze, turning hills into swathes of color. The woods around Hudson were already cancelling vestiges of green when he arrived.

It is known that native tribes once inhabited the area, and now, and then, he could sense their presence— in red grass on a hillside, a cloud shaped like smoke rising, and in silence as soft as an afternoon sleep. He came across a lake bounded by forest. Every bone within seemed to tell him he was expected to deny his role as a hunter or a victim, and that his culture forbade glances into the past as if he were already there and then, that no one could repeat their lives: "It isn't in our tradition to believe such things."

First ripples,
merely breathing disrupts the surface,
then believers who,
but for high mindedness presuming vitality before birth
must remain unseen
and fidelity to holy orders
impress duty to rearticulate their dimension,
would have found an unwavering eye
celestially borne through nigh blood transmuting indifference
into ardor wanting no other to impel conscience,
their awakening,
scurry away disillusioned.

But the moon in shadow keeping time with faint drumming across the water tells Jobe otherwise. He fingers moss and breaks off pieces of bark, smelling the damp odor underneath.

Witness thought expanding with day
and contracting with the moon's appearance,
opening when rays find a blushed hue,
losing distinction
where no contrast
can be possible at midnight.

Jobe takes off his shoes and socks and feels the soil beneath:

sacred ground.

In the lobe becoming rigid in certainty
no one can witness participating in the rituals
of a mortal race,
converting yesterday into tomorrow

  and invocation into open hearted intention
    to revive a legacy,
  waiting for a scintilla from their center
  to gleam fruitfully behind the trees
    could be seen as apostasy
     and not embodiment
      of the revelation,
   "I am the light of the world."

Vague as a whisper on an eardrum, far as light years from the sun, still alive with a presence.

     Sanguine rays
   from galaxies internecine,
   your telepathy inveigles us

    our asinine mien
   and unholy countenance

 diabolical lady who'd sew cheeks to walls,
  we'll deny your nefarious grimace,
    "I am not where I am."

Quiet as a snowflake reflecting whiteness to a snowflake, lucent as indissoluble eyes paring the surface of ultra linear gloss.

   The vector touches your brain
    and reaches back forward
   to the ruler who, disenamoured
    with your slow growth,
    implants another seed
that will hopefully grow beyond the tissue on your pate,

"If you are now, you are there
then,
and will be,
alive."

Shallow as the blaze that reaches back a minute ago, deep as a self-illuminating creature in the depths.

Righteousness challenges the fact I haven't stood here before,
felt the same grass,
experienced the same sense of foreboding
clean flesh could be replaced with a sword point
or bullet,
potential to grow
didn't fear the future because,
"I will happen again sometime,"
suffused thought
and the free gaze faintly descrying penetration
of light through the forest
divulges in quiet relief
an ordinary individual drawing breath before self-sameness.

Jobe looks between the leaves where an ant's trail makes its way homeward, a butterfly's wing brushes air sweet with flower scent, and a solitary stem sways as if blown by the lips of a holy man who has lost his way from the middle ages.

Soon
after the flowers have faded
and returned to what may be
perfect elsewhere beyond human deliverance,
the fruit recasting possibility of becoming again itself,
only slightly different, appears.

Notions of longevity are distant,
holding to a pattern
ready to acquiesce
and surrender to the next stage:

an instant requiring only an absence
and not analysis to address the absence
without which the elements
could not be distinguished one from the other.

A blaze of sunlight illuminates a profusion of growth— black berries, large as grapes, poisonous, most probably, form clusters, orange creepers thread through the entanglement, and grass grows as his waist.

The sound of running water
at the foot of rocks,
lips sutured with panic,
numinous layers interweaving and forming a cocoon
of silence,
a confusion of voices:

immanent tones portending blood spilt
by her mother kneeling,
unanswered pleas for kindness
in her breast receding

Halleluiah,
cousins

naked I dance
and pray for deliverance
from heinous stench which mouths profanity

and kills my life

God, eagle,
tender loin, sparrow head,
worm dust,
chalice:

"Befriend me."

104

STATING THE OBVIOUS

A breath of air from the south
milder than a millennium ago,
a plantation of palm
where rainforest grew luxuriant
and water dripped to the floor beneath,
the remorseless sea which pushes inland
until the mountains are the only barrier,
the rest flattened and turned to mud.

When the broken wing
is mended
the bird will fly to a high tree
and await Spring so it can express
in birdsong
the desire for a place to keep enemies from its young,
an elephant rush toward a muddy stream
when its thirst must be slaked after years
of drought,
the mountain goat descend further
into human habitation
when its food source is disrupted
by gatherers
who wish to warm their shins in winter

a star's brightness blanketed
by smoke,
a river's purity corrupted by poison

a veldt's wildlife decimated by poachers.

If I were a breathing, living entity
I would be nourished by love
and concern
for my well being

if I were a dead,
unaware thing that merely spun
on an axis
in eternal night,
no healing would be appropriate
because I would be a dead thing
in no need of life.

105

In Want of Evidence

Before the robin perched on a bottle top
and pecked for the cream,
I emerged from a sleep
where I dreamt my former self was tied
to a post and couldn't extricate
from captivity

before that,
was buried in mud and couldn't breathe

incarcerated in a dungeon,
black as the absence of light

streamed
like a rogue planet encircling a dying sun

fragrant
like lemon
in clouds uplifting in skeins

turquoise mildly understated.

When I go to the market
to buy eggs I will take the time
to peer into the shell surrounding the inside
because I have seen what has emerged
from the time
when an expansion preceded loneliness.

Point of Departure

Love
for silence

for the breathing
and repose

for the image bright
as a petal in noon rain
which, held momentarily,
fades into the night

the susurration of things
that have no bearing on the moment

attention
to the oak tree my father planted in snow,
blood in the mist,
the tapered end penetrating bordels
whose moist taste clings to an upper palate,
the unsolicited address from a Roman soldier
who,
in breaking the shaft of a battle axe,
presents a wreath to his favorite goddess

adherence
to the embryonic moon passing through shadows,
the trickster who said I could when I couldn't
and I couldn't when the planets were aligned

with growth from fertile soil,
the lemon scented arbor
where visitation
is imminent

the faith
I will return with the sense
to say something in light
and lucidity
to a friend who will understand.

107

A Friend out of Nowhere

"Are you listening?"

Darkness of the night,
a whisper through the door left ajar:

"You may not know me,
you may not care, but I love you still.

You may not understand,
you may not want
to know, but
I'll abide with you.

You may dream
of objects beyond your reach
and desire things of value you can never have,
contorting your body
in need for satiation,
but I will translate the vague murmur
in your heart
into the glow in ethereal realms.

You may be dying, frightened of the void,
but I am with you.

You may be losing your sight,
clouding aspirations of your childhood,
but I will seek
and comfort you.

The blood around the moon
will leave orbit, echoes from fields
where you lay bare
in deathly white recede,
the Muse that extracted a price
for the rare glimpse of paradise
dissolve the link
between her cortex and your brain

loneliness, the distance from me,
unintelligible

an inert pulse subject to fire
as you find what I say
has happened."

www.ingramcontent.com/pod-product-compliance
Lightning Source LLC
Chambersburg PA
CBHW051922160426
43198CB00012B/1995